DATA S_
IN CLOUD
COMPUTING,
VOLUME II

DATA SECURITY IN CLOUD COMPUTING, VOLUME II

GIULIO D'AGOSTINO

 MOMENTUM PRESS
ENGINEERING

First published in 2019 by
Momentum Press®, LLC
222 East 46th Street, New York, NY 10017
www.momentumpress.net

ISBN-13: 978-1-94944-923-5 (print)
ISBN-13: 978-1-94944-924-2 (e-book)

Momentum Press Computer Engineering Foundations, Currents, and Trajectories Collection

Cover and interior design by S4Carlisle Publishing Services Private Ltd., Chennai, India

First edition: 2019

10 9 8 7 6 5 4 3 2 1

Printed in the United States of America

Dedication

To my wife Eimear for standing beside me throughout my career and writing this book.

ABSTRACT

Cloud computing has already been adopted by many organizations and people because of its advantages of economy, reliability, scalability and guaranteed quality of service amongst others. Readers will learn specifics about software as a service (SaaS), platform as a service (PaaS), infrastructure as a service (IaaS), server and desktop virtualization, and much more.

This book covers not only information protection in cloud computing security and risk management, but also the plan, management, and in-depth implementation details needed to migrate existing applications to the cloud. Readers will have a greater comprehension of cloud engineering and the actions required to rapidly reap its benefits while at the same time lowering IT implementation risk. The book's content is ideal for users wanting to migrate to the cloud, IT professionals seeking an overview on cloud fundamentals, and computer science students who will build cloud solutions for testing purposes.

KEYWORDS

Amazon Web Services; API; Azure; BaaS; cloud computing; computer engineering and science; Google Cloud; Java; MySQL; Node.js; SaaS; SQL

Contents

LIST OF FIGURES

LIST OF TABLES

LIST OF ABBREVIATIONS

API	Application Programming Interface
BYOT	Bring Your Own Technology
CAIQ	Cloud Evaluation Initiative Questionnaire
CCs	Cloud Clients
CIO	Chief Information Officer
CSA	Cloud Security Alliance
CSP	Cloud Service Provider
DDoS	Distributed Denial of Service
DoS	Denial of Service
DR	Disaster Recovery
ENISA	European Network and Information Security Agency
EU	European Union
FSI	Financial Services Institutions
IaaS	Infrastructure-as-a-Service
ISP	Internet Service Providers
IT	Information Technology
MAC	Media Access Control
NAT	Network Address Translation
NFS	Network File Systems
NIST	National Institute of Science and Technology
PaaS	Platform-as-a-Service
PII	Personally Identifiable Information
PocT	Policy as a Trust Management Technique
PrdT	Prediction as a Trust Management Technique
RecT	Recommendation as a Trust Management Technique
RepT	Reputation as a Trust Management Technique
RMF	Risk Management Frame
SA	Support Arrangement
SaaS	Software-as-a-Service
SLA	Service Level Agreement
SNMP	Simple Network Management Protocol
VM	Virtual Machine

ACKNOWLEDGMENTS

First and foremost, I would like to thank my family and friends for always standing by me. I also thank Nigel Wyatt, Michael Weiss (Griffith College Dublin), Gabriel Grecco (photography), and the Momentum Press team for the support and inspiration.

INTRODUCTION

This second volume of my series of works dedicated to Data Security in Cloud Computing acts as a professional benchmark, as well as a practitioner's guide to today's most complete and concise view of cloud computing security. It offers coverage on cloud computing security concepts, technology, and practice as they relate to based technologies, and to recent advancements. It investigates practical answers to a wide assortment of cloud computing protection issues.

The primary audience for this book consists of engineers/students interested in monitoring and analyzing specific, measurable cloud computing protection environments, which may include infrastructure or transportation systems, mechanical systems, seismic events, and underwater environments. This book will also be useful for safety and related professionals interested in tactical surveillance and mobile cloud computing protection target classification and monitoring. This thorough reference and practitioner's short book is also of significance to students in upper-division undergraduate and graduate-level classes in cloud computing security.

CHAPTER 7

SECURE CLOUD ARCHITECTURE

The Internet has provided seamless connectivity of computing nodes across continents; hence the computing paradigm in the beginning of the nineteenth century has developed into cloud computing. The elements of cloud computing architecture are all hardware and software, needed for the delivery of cloud computing solutions (NIST and U.S. Department of Commerce 2013). Furthermore, these components of a cloud computing architecture are coordinated into front-end platforms or cloud customers, backend platforms such as servers and storage devices, along with a route connecting front to the rear end to get cloud-based solutions. This route is the network, which can be either the public (Internet) or a private community, as shown in Figure 7.1. The role of this network is to give services. The general public cloud tools are made available to cloud-based customers through Internet service providers (ISPs).

Security can be broken in either or both the cloud infrastructure or across the Internet. Cloud computing providers offer elasticity, quick provisioning and discharging of resources, resource pooling, and higher bandwidth access, but with higher security risks. Just as data facilities were both business and technical constructs to support data processing needs of businesses, the cloud in a sense is more like a business construct, since the security and privacy in the cloud are managed more or less from the cloud service providers.

The public cloud computing service users no longer own the infrastructure; hence, the data security has to be managed by the cloud service providers. This is a change in paradigm, which also calls for redefining the governance of both privacy and security. This in no way indicates that consumers of cloud providers do not need to check their information privacy and security handling process, but should have a service level agreement (SLA) with all the cloud service providers and identify suitable levels of protection that are compliant with the state in which they operate.

Risk management needs to factor the dangers specific to different installation cloud models and devise solutions to mitigate those dangers. Data confidentiality, integrity, and its accessibility in a cloud installation model are somewhat more susceptible to risk compared to some noncloud

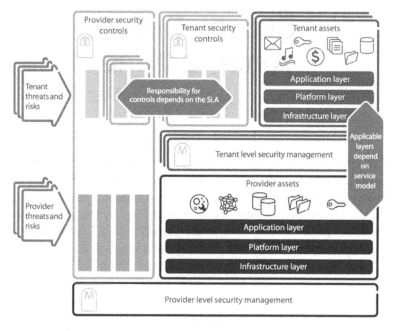

Figure 7.1. Cloud computing structure

Figure 7.2. Just how secure is your cloud?

deployment model. Secure cloud computing architecture has to be scalable, to react to most insider and outsider threats as well as natural disasters.

Next, we itemize lots of safety risks connected with the deployment of cloud computing systems. These risks have to be addressed by the service provider and stated in the SLA. The client must know the full implications of the dangers because the service suppliers are offering the service to their clients required to safeguard their clients' information (Cloud Security Alliance 2011):

- Governance: Considering that the user doesn't manage the computing infrastructure, the management of security and privacy is considerably looser, but has to be compliant with the local state and federal regulations.
- Ambiguity in governance: The cloud service provider must cover the privacy and safety requirements of most of its customers, who could differ in their needs as to what constitutes minimal governance.
- Regulatory compliance: Consumers of cloud computing have to offer the security of their clients' data stored at the service provider facility, which in turn demands that the cloud service providers have appropriate certifications per state regulations.
- Security incidents: Detection, reporting, and management of security breaches must be transparent and documented immediately to the consumers of computing.
- Information security: Cloud computing service providers need to ensure maintenance of mission-critical data from corruption or unauthorized access and supply detailed data backup processes to prevent compromises to the integrity and confidentiality of data in transit to and from a cloud supplier (man-in-the-middle).
- Information deletion: In the event of termination of SLA, the consumer must explicitly demand the data storage medium entirely and irrevocably deletes the consumer data. This scenario has legal ramifications in the event the data are then sold in a secondary market.
- Business failure: The cloud support supplier may file bankruptcy, and consequently fail to continue to give access to sources to their clients, which would adversely affect the company cycles of the consumers.
- Service interruptions: Network service providers are the backbone of cloud computing, who provide the connectivity between the cloud consumers and cloud support provided.

Safety and privacy issues faced by the cloud customers require them to assess the risk and its management in the cloud environment, mitigating these risks. Of course, the most crucial advantage provided by cloud computing is the reduction of business costs.

7.1. GOVERNANCE AND COMPREHENSIVE RISK ANALYSIS

Most companies have well-established security goals, strategies, and policies consistent with compliance needs to guard their intellectual property and their customers' data. Many safety elements come into play; however, the four most critical components are shown in Figure 7.3. Information and its transmission must take place through bonded channels. Application and storage safety must be preserved by the cloud service provider. Figure 7.4 illustrates the role performed by a safety agent, who is

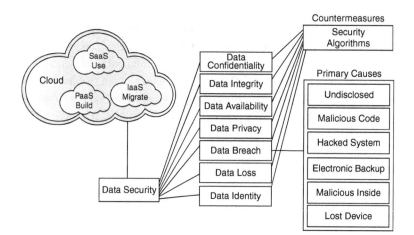

Figure 7.3. Four safety elements

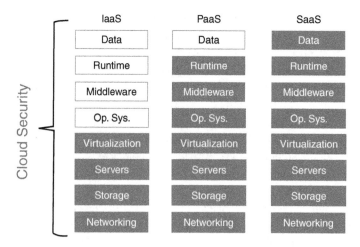

Figure 7.4. The role performed by a safety agent

a middleman between a cloud supplier and cloud client. A security agent would act on behalf of both the cloud service provider and cloud client. A cloud auditor can also provide auditing services. An individual cloud computing client would need the services of a security broker, who might also act as a legal advisor to interpret the SLA.

The framework for security policies is designed based on the hazard analysis prediction and its impact on business earnings in case the resources are compromised. Security and privacy needs in cloud computing do vary from conventional IT environment, but what is common to both is the impact of a security violation on corporate assets. In cloud computing, a breach of security wouldn't impact just one cloud computing customer, its effects may be far-reaching as other customers' safety might also be breached. As a result, the frame for security control policy must factor in support for a number of customers.

Cloud customers need to comprehend the risk they're subjected to, and therefore they will need to impose their security controls along with the one supplied from the cloud supplier, because not all of the cloud clients need the same level of service as regards infrastructure, software, and platform as a service. As part of general governance, a cloud support provider would need to indemnify their clients in the event the breach in security occurred because of willful negligence or act on the part of the service supplier. Most cloud service providers have several locations for their data centers spread over technical boundaries, and this also has to be taken into account when a business signs up for cloud hosting services; Figure 7.5 shows a situation where a cloud client is attempting to access distributed data among the cloud supplier's data centers. In this case, the information in each data center is subjected to the regulations and laws of the country it's situated in, which raises security concerns on how data are managed in those countries or whether it is in transit. This is highly critical

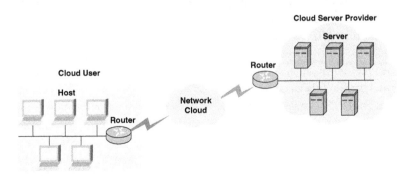

Figure 7.5. Cloud user and Service Provider

since privacy laws are not uniform across geopolitical boundaries, and it might have far-reaching consequences if the assets were compromised.

The cloud service supplier must create audit reports of their solutions on a regular basis, which they need to share with their customers as mentioned in the SLA. The audit report should itemize customers' logs of all data processing and data storage access activities, including any apparent anomalous action.

More frequent security breaches mean that service providers must now be mandated to apply compliance regulations. Not every nation has the same compliance regulations, and this could be of significant consequence to consumers.

Consumer information of any type, such as unstructured or structured, and stored in any format (encrypted or unencrypted) on media would be the life and blood of any company. Of course, when a company chooses to subscribe to the assistance of a cloud computing provider, it has to know about exposure to risk regarding their information. The company may decide to move only noncritical data to the cloud and maintain critical data locally within their IT infrastructure, thus reducing the risk factor. As time passes, corporations may decide this branch to be not practical, and hence decide to transfer all of their corporate information to the cloud. The cloud computing support provider probably has the policy to disperse the client data in their multiple data centers. The inherent nature of cloud computing is just one of distribution to overcome one point of collapse, so the customer has access to their information on a 24/7 basis.

Cloud computing has improved the reach of safety to both data that are static and information that is moving along the network; consequently, a corporation must make an analysis of its information assets. Data (structured in addition to unstructured) should be categorized into data sets, each set corresponding to specific purposes, which would signify business processes associated with various departments within a given company. Every one of those departments would have certain processing rights to all those business processes, and hence into the information collections. Here we need to define security privileges utilizing some reflexive algorithm assigned to each of the business processes, and thus to the data collections; the chief information officer (CIO) would have the maximum degree of privilege to all the data collections.

The reflexive algorithm also identifies the branches that have shared access (inclusive) to data collections, and the ones that have a private entrance, under accessibility management. Thus, the safety policy is now defined using the reflexive algorithm, and safety controls are employed. The next step is to put up the monitoring of business processes. Security policy characterized

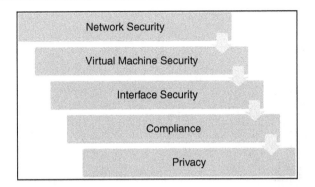

Figure 7.6. Example of compliance architecture

and controllers implemented should ensure the privacy of data sets consistent with local compliance regulations (Figure 7.6). Of course, the cloud computing service provider would also need to have in place security controls to safeguard their consumers' information sets. Consumers need to decide as it pertains to the information sets that should be encrypted. This decision would depend on the nature of the data, and how often data are obtained. With the present encryption algorithm, data would have to be decrypted on the fly for processing, thus adding cost and latency to the company cost factor.

In this section, we propose a matrix (Table 7.1) to assess the risk associated with a cloud computing service. In the first three columns, we identify the type of threat, and how this threat could exploit the vulnerability to the assets in question. Present safeguards are given for each threat, and then the consequences are listed with the associated levels of severity, likelihood, as well as danger.

Figure 7.7 (case study) shows a schematic diagram of an internal LAN security infrastructure of a cloud computing supplier. Observe the placement of a perimeter router placed facing an outside firewall. The interior LAN architecture reveals the installation of an internal firewall to secure the community further.

In this chapter, we analyzed aspects of cloud computing security, as it is an essential building block where cloud services are constructed. A cloud computing support provider must offer an SLA to its prospective client seeking to register for cloud services. The SLA is the most significant document that could provide a level of satisfaction to the cloud client in the event of a breach of security. We must point out that management and evaluation of safety risks are equally dynamic processes, and since vulnerabilities are found, a guard has to be reassessed; thus, control of security is an ever-evolving procedure.

Table 7.1. Risk assessment matrix

Threat (what could happen?)	Threat agent	Vulnerability	Existing safeguards	Consequence	Severity	Likelihood	Risk

Interactive network breach	1. Targeted attacker
	2. Script kiddie
	3. Unauthorized internal employee
		1. Via Internet
		2. Via internal physical connection to network
			1. IDS equipment and software
			2. Firewall rules and segmented network
			3. Physical safeguards preventing unauthorized direct access to network from inside the building
				1. Monetary effects
				  a. Regulatory penalties
				  b. Loss of customer revenue
				2. Loss of data/service
					High	Medium	Medium

Malware is introduced into the environment	1. Internal employees (unwittingly) 2. Internal employees (knowingly) 3. Contractors	1. E-mail attachments 2. USB drives 3. Data uploads 4. FTP feeds	1. Employee security awareness training 2. Removal of USB ports on client machines 3. Data validation performed after uploads 4. Uploads are performed via web programs rather than directly interactively	1. Monetary effects a. Regulatory penalties 2. Loss of data/service			

Scenario	Threats	Vulnerability	Existing controls	Impact			
Natural disaster destroys data center	1. Earthquake 2. Tornado 3. Flooding	Data center operations could be interrupted, availability of systems and data could be compromised	1. Backups are sent offsite daily for all critical systems 2. Offsite disaster recovery (DR) contract in place	1. Monetary effects a. Regulatory penalties 2. Loss of data/service	High	Low	Low
Case study: Hospital quarantined due to outbreak	1. Disease	1. Physical backup media could be prevented from being sent offsite. 2. Associates may not be able to access the worksite to administer the environment	1. Offsite backups are sent electronically to a hosted vault 2. Administrative staff can access the network with VPN using two-factor authentication	1. Loss of recovery capability 2. Loss of administrative access to servers/network 3. Loss of physical	Medium	Low	Low

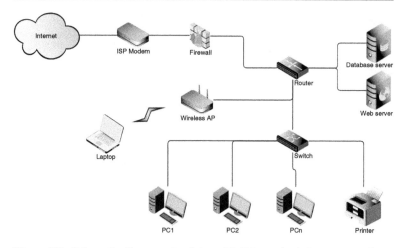

Figure 7.7. Schematic diagram of an internal LAN security infrastructure of a cloud computing supplier

REFERENCES

Cloud Security Alliance. 2011. "Security Guidance for Critical Areas of Focus in Cloud Computing V3.0." https://cloudsecurityalliance.org/guidance/csaguide.v3.0.pdf

NIST and U.S. Department of Commerce. 2013. "NIST Cloud Computing Standards Roadmap," Special Publication 500-291, version 2.

CHAPTER 8

RISK AND TRUST ASSESSMENT

The trust connection between cloud clients (CCs) and cloud hosting support providers (CSPs) needs to be established until CCs transfer their data systems into the cloud. This necessitates an in-depth comprehension of related risks. Moreover, regulations associated with information security, financial reporting, etc., demand particular requirements that need to be complied with when outsourcing business processes to third parties, such as CSPs. However, the majority of the CCs, notably small and medium companies, might not have sufficient knowledge in doing such evaluations at a suitable level since they might not always employ a professional for this and also too little transparency is inherent to the operations of the CSPs.

A CC includes a unique challenge in hazard assessment in contrast to traditional information technology (i.e., aside from cloud) clients. CSPs usually maintain the places, structure, and information about the safety of the server farms and data centers confidential from CCs.

Additionally, the abstract view of this cloud is just one of the benefits promised from the cloud theory: CCs don't have to get an in-depth understanding of the technical specifics of this cloud. Because of this, it's tougher for a CC to evaluate each of the dangers and vulnerabilities. Notice that the dangers aren't just associated with safety problems but also to support outages, and CSPs must reevaluate the issues to resolve when risks are accomplished. A CC must rely on the regular procedures of this CSP for handling the infrastructure suitably. As stated by the CCs' safety dynamics, managing the CCs' problems in a timely fashion, discovering, recovering, and reporting the safety and support outage events correctly is a combination of strong risk management and security processes in place. These uncertainties increase danger and indicate that the CCs must trust the CSPs (Rousseau et al. 1998).

Both trust and risk have been extensively studied in a variety of contexts for centuries. Risk management, and especially hazard assessment for IT, has also become a favorite research topic for many decades (Kaplan and Garrick 1981). In this chapter, we offer a questionnaire on cloud hazard assessment made by different organizations, in addition to hazard and trust models designed for the cloud.

We'd like to begin by clarifying several phrases we use later in our chapter:

- Threat: A threat is the possible cause of an embarrassing incident, which might lead to harm to an individual system, individual, or business.
- Vulnerability: Vulnerability is the weakness of a controller that may be exploited by a threat.
- Asset: An asset is something of value to your business, which may be concrete (e.g., a construction, pc hardware) or abstract (e.g., understanding, expertise, know-how, data, applications, information).
- Control: A control prevents or lessens the likelihood of safety, privacy, or support episode (preventive or deterrent control), suggests that an event has happened (detective management), or reduces the damage brought on by an episode, that is, reduces or restricts the effect (surgical management). The identification of this individual doesn't have to be direct. As an instance, there may be several individuals whose name is John and have been created on a particular date, but there might be just one John with this arrival date and who is functioning in a specific firm.
- Data topic: A data subject is an individual or company who's the subject of personal information.
- Incident: An incident is an event that leads to safety, privacy, or support violation/outage; instances are confidential information leakages following an assault, private data collection without proper approval from the data issues, or information that can't be retrieved following a hardware failure, respectively.
- Event: An event is something that produces a vulnerability that could be exploited by a threat to undermine a person's strength(s). It's imperative not to confuse occasion with an event; for example, losing an accessibility badge is a safety event. When an individual employs the missing badge to go into a building without consent, then it's an incident.
- Security episode: A safety incident can be described as a single attack or a set of attacks which can be distinguished from other people by the system of assault, identity of attackers, victims, web sites, goals, timing, etc.

- Privacy episode: A solitude incident may be an intentional or accidental violation of permission obtained from the data control for the data issues or even a breach of the appropriate data security regulatory frame. A solitude incident may be the result of a service or security episode. By way of instance, a data control utilizes information for purposes not initially declared; an individual gains access to personally identifiable information; private data are moved to third parties without permission. Notice that we count the events brought on by denial of service attacks as support events because their outcomes have been service outages.

The following section is on hazard analysis, evaluation, and direction where we establish risk and complications of the connections and differences between hazard analysis, appraisal, and management. In Chapter 6, we have presented a recent research completed for assessing the threats and vulnerabilities, including the Cloud Security Alliance (CSA) initiative, to examine the best threats against the cloud and also to acquire a better insight to how well the CSPs are ready for them. The CNIL ran a privacy threat assessment for the cloud recently. CNIL's work goes farther by introducing some steps to decrease the risks to acceptable levels. Chapter 6 was about trust and risk models. At precisely the same phase, we also present two versions developed by A4Cloud, and it will be a European Framework Seven job. The first is that the cloud embraced hazard assessment model (CARAM), a qualitative design that adapts ENISA and also CNIL frameworks for particular CSP–CC pairs based on controllers employed by CSPs and resources that the CC intends to store or process from a cloud. The second version is known as the common threat and trust version (JRTM), which will be a quantitative model based on the CSP operation information.

A risk is defined as the impact of uncertainty on goals in these criteria. This means that if we're sure about the result of a procedure, there's entirely no risk associated with this procedure. The dangers can be correlated with not just adverse outcomes (risks) but also favorable outcomes (chances). In such criteria, missing a chance can be treated as a hazard. Therefore, uncertainty is the principal element in hazard analysis; lots of resources for doubt may exist. However, we could group them into two broad categories: epistemic and aleatory.

Epistemic uncertainties are the result of a deficiency of knowledge. Since the cloud ecosystem and solutions in the cloud grow, this group of doubts will decrease or proceed to the aleatory uncertainty domain name. Aleatory is derived from the Latin term "Alea," which means "rolling a stunt." Therefore, aleatory doubts are based upon the inherent randomness of this processor phenomenon under analysis for hazard analysis. Also, it suggests that the information available will suffice for construction opportunities or frequency distributions.

When doubts may be treated as aleatory, a qualitative hazard analysis (Kaplan and Garrick 1981) could be completed. Three inquiries are answered through a quantitative hazard analysis:

- The probability pi of all si (i.e., the likelihood that the situation is accomplished)
- The result xi of si

The likelihood of a situation relies on the occurrence of vulnerabilities, threats that may exploit the vulnerabilities, the consciousness of risks about the vulnerabilities, as well as the capacities and willingness of these dangers to exploit the vulnerabilities. The most important thing is that a threat is in nature the product of risks, vulnerabilities, and also the results of the exploitation of vulnerabilities from the dangers (i.e., the effects of danger).

When doubts are for the most part from the epistemic domain if chosen, a qualitative hazard analysis may also be conducted. For qualitative hazard analysis, a qualitative scale for chances, like almost certain, probable, possible, unlikely, infrequent, and impacts, such as critical, necessary, moderate, small, insignificant, is employed (Cooper et al. 2014). Notice that we use the expression likelihood rather than the probability for qualitative hazard analysis. Risk understanding for the exact same situation may be different from person to person from time to time since the probabilities and effects may be different for different individuals at various times. This can be known as a perceived danger. On the flip side, the absolute danger is the same for everybody and every moment. It's not simple to calculate the absolute danger because a person's absolute risk is the perceived danger for somebody else. Perceived danger can be quite often called comparative danger in the literature; however, in our chapter, we'll use the term relative risk otherwise. Relative risk is the danger of a plan of action in contrast to that of the following plan of action.

A good instance of relative risk is the chance of utilizing the cloud rather than of your infrastructure and applications. Another illustration is the danger of getting services from a single CSP rather than another CSP. By way of instance, event tree analysis is an inductive (i.e., bottom-up) method to assess the ramifications of working or neglected systems provided that an event has happened. On the flip side, fault tree analysis is a deductive (i.e., top-down) technique based on operating in the upper-level undesired occasion to comprehend what might cause that collapse before reaching the primary cause for each one of the branches of the fault tree.

Risk evaluation is a systematic evaluation of a hazard scenario to comprehend its probability/likelihood and effects. The next step following a hazard analysis is hazard assessment, which is briefly described as analyzing a risk situation (high risk, moderate risk, low hazard, etc.) according to its probability/likelihood and effects. Risk management is a process of identifying, assessing, analyzing, and communicating hazard situations and mitigating them as necessary. This hierarchy of risk evaluation, evaluation, and management is represented in Figure 8.1. Mitigation

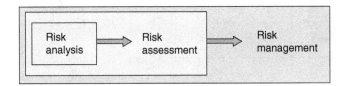

Figure 8.1. Risk control strategy

strategies can be made for mitigating the causes or results of the threat scenarios according to a number of these approaches: risk acceptance, risk avoidance, risk limit, and risk transference. Risk approval doesn't lessen the likelihood or effect of a risk situation. Since the price of avoidance, limit, or transference isn't inexpensive or too high in contrast to the effects of the situation, the threat is approved in the expectation it won't happen. Risk avoidance is the opposite of approval; the activity subject to the threat scenario isn't taken in any way to prevent it. Alternatively, reduction plans might be implemented or ready to restrict the causes or the results of a hazard situation. Last, the threat can be moved to another party, like an insurance provider, at the cost of whatever the price tag is for your transport.

For cloud hazard evaluation, the CSA listing of the best threats is a significant source, to begin with. CSA conducted a poll among the specialists and stakeholders to get an insight into their understanding on the dangers against the cloud and printed the results of a document titled "The infamous nine: cloud computing top dangers in 2013." A previous version of the same document was released in 2010.

From the record, nine dangers selected as the best threats are introduced at the priority sequence determined by the very same specialists who contributed to the 2013 document. For every hazard, besides its description, the data portrayed in Figure 8.2 can also be given: what support versions this threat can influence, what proportion of those specialists consider it as important, what its position was at the 2010 poll, and the way it's perceived as a hazard—real or perceived. We do not elaborate on each of those "notorious nine" farther in this chapter since the titles of these dangers are

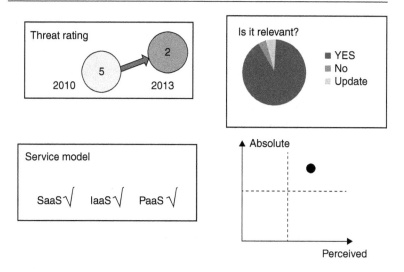

Figure 8.2. Cloud hazard assessment models

self-explanatory and our chapter is not about the risks but cloud hazard assessment models. Further explanations of all these dangers are seen at Ezell et al. (2010) and in several other chapters in this publication.

The 2013 CSA's notorious four record comprises the dangers in the specified order below:

1. Data reduction
2. Account or support visitors hijacking
3. Abuse of cloud providers
4. Shared technology vulnerabilities

Aside from the record about the infamous nine, another significant source that may be somewhat helpful for cloud hazard analysis is the consensus assessment initiative questionnaire (CAIQ) (CSA 2014), a survey ready for CSPs from CSA. This intends to address a few of those infamous nine "inadequate due diligence." The CAIQ incorporates many queries categorized into command classes listed below:

- Compliance
- Data governance
- Center safety
- Human resources safety
- Information safety
- Legal
- Operations direction
- Risk direction

- Release direction
- Resilience
- Safety structure

The questionnaires answered by several CSPs can be found by any-body. The CSA's Security, Trust & Assurance Registry (STAR) database has grown a source to understand how well a specific CSP is ready to handle several dangers. It indicates estimating the amount of danger on the grounds of a chance of a hazard situation mapped against the projected ad-verse effect, which is also the gist of the hazard formulation by others from the literature (Cayirci 2013; Cayirci et al. 2014; Ezell et al. 2010; ISACA 2014; ISO/IEC 31010 2014; Kaplan and Garrick 1981). Though ENISA's guidelines are particular for cloud computing, it's a generic framework that doesn't supply a way to map the particulars of CSPs and CCs into the 35 threat scenarios listed in the report (ENISA 2014). ENISA's risk situ-ations are grouped into four classes: organizational and policy, technical, legal, and other situations not specific to computing.

The chances of all those situations and their business impact are de-cided in consultation with a specialist team.

The scale of impact and likelihood has five different classes involving very low and very significant. By way of instance, the very first incident scenario from the organizational and policy group is P1—seller lock-in, and its chances and effect are awarded as HIGH and MEDIUM, respectively. Afterward, the likelihood (probability) and substantial impact (effect) values depending on the specialists are changed into the hazard levels for every episode scenario, according to a risk matrix using a scale between 0 and 8 as shown in Figure 8.3. Last, the hazard levels are mapped into some qualitative scale. All 35 episode scenarios are connected using a subset of both vulnerabilities and resources.

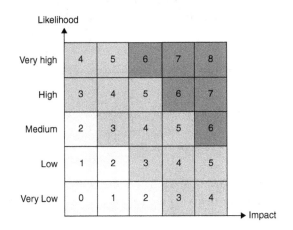

Figure 8.3. Risk matrix using a scale between 0 and 8

As an example, the incident situation P1—seller lock-in is related to vulnerabilities V13 (shortage of conventional technology and alternatives), V31 (lack of completeness and transparency concerning usage), V46 (poor supplier selection), V47 (lack of provider redundancy), and resources A1 (company standing). A CC can evaluate the risk level associated with a situation qualitatively and comprehend what sort of vulnerabilities and resources are linked to each situation by evaluation (ENISA 2014).

Nonetheless, these values represent educated guesses within a variety of common cloud deployments and also with no exact semantics. ENISA's framework could be categorized as a standard qualitative inductive hazard analysis framework for computing. CNIL's methodology is comparable to ENISA's frame using these differences: it's a risk assessment centered on privacy dangers in cloud computing systems. It's still generic and doesn't distinguish CSPs or CCs. It features not just a test on the amount of danger for the recorded episode scenarios (i.e., feared occasions) but also some steps. Additionally, it assesses the residual dangers for the event these steps are implemented. Based on CNIL, a hazard employs the vulnerabilities of resources, like computers, information storage, and amenities, to change or to get access to the primary assets like private data, which affects the proprietor of these main assets. The final result is known as a dreaded event. This relation among the elements of a threat is portrayed in Figure 8.4.

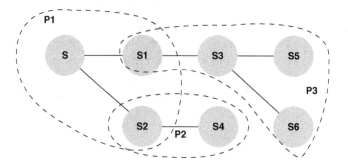

Figure 8.4. Relation among the elements of a threat

Notice that CNIL is a danger assessment just for privacy-related feared occasions. CNIL also categorizes the main assets associated with such events into two categories:

- Procedures: They process the personal data or data needed by the procedures for notifying the data issues, receiving their approval, letting the practice of their rights of opposition, access, correction, and deletion.

- Personal information: They would be the information used by the procedures that fall in the principal strength category. Thus, they're not just the information processed but additionally the information needed for processing the personal information.

CNIL decides the dangers against solitude in the cloud as:

- People who belong to the business: user-friendly, a computer expert, etc.
- Individuals from outside the business: recipient, supplier, rival, accredited third party, a government company, human action, etc.
- Nonhuman resources: computer virus, natural catastrophe, flammable substances, outbreak, rodents, etc.

Very similar to many other hazard assessments, CNIL calculates the amount of risk based on its severity and likelihood. It first assesses and assigns the values for both likelihood and seriousness and sums them to figure out the amount of danger as specified in Equation 8.1. This differs from many different approaches that mimic the dangerous situations as a product of chance and impact but less a sum of those.

$$\text{Amount of danger} = \text{seriousness} + \text{chances} \qquad (8.1)$$

CNIL utilizes a scale with four principles: minimal, restricted, relevant, and maximum. Additionally, it provides the precise definitions of what these values mean in a variety of contexts (i.e., the amount of identification for private information, the prejudicial impact of dreaded events, vulnerabilities of encouraging assets, and capacities of hazard sources).

For every feared occasion, these parameters have been assigned values, and also the seriousness and chances are calculated using Equation 8.2.

$$\text{Likelihood} = \text{vulnerabilities} + \text{capacities} \qquad (8.2)$$

The outcomes of the equations are mapped to qualitative values:

<5 Negligible
$=5$ Restricted
$=6$ Important
>6 Maximum

This practice ends together with all the matrix in Figure 8.5, which depicts the amount of risk for every emphasized event. CNIL proceeds with recommendations (steps) on how best to take care of these dangers

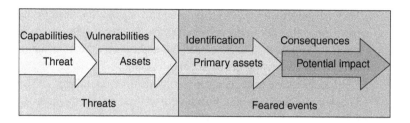

Figure 8.5. The matrix that depicts the amount of risk for every emphasized event

such that they may be changed to the left and right down at the amount of risk matrix. Then, it reassesses the degree of dangers—known as residual dangers—and justifies why they are okay following this therapy.

Risk and hope modeling from cloud computing standpoint have attracted scientists lately (Pearson 2012; Rashidi and Movahhedinia 2012), and "hope for a support" is introduced into the cloud industry model. Standardized trust versions are necessary for confirmation and assurance of responsibility, but not one of the high number of current trust models so far is sufficient for its cloud environment (Li and Ping 2009). There are lots of trust models that try to adopt a few of the variables characterized by Marsh (1994) and Banerjee et al. (2005); there are also lots of trust evaluation mechanisms that aim to quantify them. Definition of hope could be a beginning point for simulating it. This definition doesn't fully capture all of the dynamics of confidence, like the probabilities that the trustee will conduct a specific activity and won't engage in opportunistic behavior (Pearson 2012). Additionally, there are soft and hard facets of confidence (Osterwalder 2001; Singh and Morley 2009; Wang and Lin 2008). The hard part of confidence depends upon the safety measures. Like authentication and encryption, gentle trust relies on facets like brand loyalty and standing. Ryan et al. (2011) introduce not just safety but also accountability and auditability as components that affect CC confidence in cloud computing.

- Information place: CCs understand where their information is in fact found.
- Analysis: CCs can inquire into the status and place of the information.
- Data segregation: Others separate statistics of every CC.
- Accessibility: CCs can get their information at any moment.
- Backup and recovery: the CSP has mechanics and capability to recuperate from catastrophic failures and isn't vulnerable to disasters.
- Long-term qualifications: the CSP has been doing above the necessary standards for quite a while.

The writers mathematically examine the results of a questionnaire responded by 72 CCs to look into the perception of their CCs about the significance of the parameters previously. Following the investigation, backup and retrieval generate the most potent effect on CCs' confidence in cloud computing followed by accessibility, privileged CC accessibility, regulatory compliance, long-term viability, and information location. Their poll revealed that info segregation and analysis have a poor effect on CCs' hope of computing. Khan and Malluhi (2013) suggest committing controls to CCs so that they could track the parameters described previously (Rashidi and Movahhedinia 2012). They categorize these controllers into five broad categories: controls on information saved, data through processing, applications, regulatory compliance, and charging.

The techniques that have to be designed for all these controls include remote monitoring, prevention of access to staying data, protected outsourcing, data intrusion, machine-readable regulations and SLA, automated reasoning about compliance, an automated group of real-time intake data, and also the capacity of this CC to restrain their own usage/ bill. Although these are methods that have been developed for the two cloud computing and other functions, many CSPs still require time for their execution, installation, and maturity. Besides, they need a long time and experience by CCs. Also, using these controllers for all of the services at a cloud support mash-up might not always be sensible.

Reliability trust is described as the likelihood of success and contained from the risk-based decision-making procedure for a trade. Yudistira et al. (2007) introduce hope for analyzing risks on the grounds of their organizational setting of an individual system. The trustworthiness of celebrities the achievement of a system is dependent upon impacts on the likelihood of a risk situation, and this connection is addressed (Yudistira et al. 2007). CARAM is a qualitative design that contrasts the methodology and evaluations created by ENISA and also CNIL to evaluate the threat for a specified CSP–CC pair. For adapting the chances and impact assessments created within an ENISA report into a CSP and a CC, CARAM utilizes the information regarding the CSP accessible STAR and resources possessed by the CC, respectively.

The JRTM (Cayirci 2013; Cayirci and Oliviera n.d.) is just another version manufactured by A4Cloud. It's a quantitative risk assessment model that calculates the likelihood of privacy, security, and support dangers based on the CSP operation information. It computes the likelihood that an event happens and the likelihood that an occasion is removed before it turns into an event, also subtracting the latter in the former. For performance information, JRTM counts on the episode reports provided by CSPs; it also includes a penalty strategy for those CSPs which don't report correctly.

Many frameworks have been suggested to help users in support selection based on many different standards like QoS functionality (Tran and Tsuji 2008; Wang et al. 2006), confidence and standing level (Maximilien and Singh 2004; Paradesi, Doshi, and Swaika 2009; Vu, Hauswirth, and Aberer 2005; Wang et al. 2009; Xu et al. 2007), and solitude (Costante, Paci, and Zannone 2013). CARAM and JRTM may also be utilized as a service choice instrument.

Risk and hope are crucial issues for cloud providers and are closely associated with one another. From the literature, trust is the principal barrier for prospective customers until they adopt cloud solutions. This necessitates an in-depth comprehension of cloud dangers. Thus, various organizations like CSA, ENISA, and CNIL completed research to get a better insight into them. CSA also maintains a record of questionnaires called STAR. Many CSPs replied the CAIQ and enrolled their replies in STAR. Both the infamous two and STAR are significant resources for cloud hazard evaluation. In 2009, ENISA also ran a cloud hazard assessment, which was a qualitative analysis on the probability and effects of 35 episode cases. Its research covers safety, privacy, and support dangers and explains the vulnerabilities and resources associated with each scenario. In its report, CNIL introduces a few steps to decrease the privacy dangers. ENISA's and CNIL's hazard evaluations are generic and don't distinguish the CSPs or CCs.

There are additional risks and trust versions such as CARAM and JRTM, which evaluate the dangers of a CSP for a CC. CARAM is a qualitative model according to ENISA's hazard assessment and STAR. JRTM is a qualitative model which computes the probability of safety, privacy, and support dangers in line with the incident reports provided by CSPs. Various danger and trust-based service choice schemes which use versions such as CARAM and JRTM are offered for encouraging CCs in locating the cloud solutions which match their risk landscape most excellent from the literature. Our chapter provides a questionnaire on those models and strategies.

REFERENCES

Banerjee, S., C. Mattmann, N. Medvidovic, and L. Golubchik. 2005. Leveraging architectural models to inject trust into software systems. In *Proceedings of the 2005 Workshop on Software Engineering for Secure Systems—Building Trustworthy Applications*. New York, NY: ACM, pp. 1–7.

Cayirci, E. 2013. "A Joint Trust and Risk Model for MSaaS Mashups." In *Proceedings of the 2013 Winter Simulation Conference*, ed. R. Pasupathy, S.-H. Kim,

A. Tolk, R. Hill, and M.E. Kuhl. Piscataway, NJ: Institute of Electrical and Electronics Engineers, Inc., pp. 1347–58.

Cayirci, E., A. Garaga, A.S. Oliveira, and Y. Roudier. 2014. "Cloud Adopted Risk Assessment Model." In *Proceedings of the 2014 IEEE/ACM 7th International Conference on Utility and Cloud Computing (UCC '14)*. Washington, DC: IEEE Computer Society, pp. 908–913.

Cayirci, E., and A.S. Oliviera. n.d. "Modelling Trust and Risk for Cloud Services." *IEEE Transactions on Cloud Computing* (submitted).

Cooper, D., P. Bosnich, S. Grey, G. Purdy, G. Raymond, P. Walker, and M. Wood. 2014. *Project Risk Management Guidelines: Managing Risk with ISO 31000 and IEC 62198*. 2nd ed. Chichester, England: Wiley. ISBN 978-1-118-84913-2.

Costante, E., F. Paci, and N. Zannone. 2013. Privacy-aware Web Service Composition and Ranking. *Proceedings of the 2013 IEEE International Conference on Web Services*, June 28 to July 3, pp. 131–138, Santa Clara, CA.

CSA. 2014. "Consensus Assessment Initiative Questionnaire." https://downloads.cloudsecurityalliance.org/initiatives/cai/CAIQ_v3.0.1_Info_Sheet.pdf

CSA. 2014. "The Notorious Nine Cloud Computing Top Threats in 2013." https://downloads.cloudsecurityalliance.org/initiatives/top_threats/The_Notorious_Nine_Cloud_Computing_Top_Threats_in_2013.pdf

ENISA. 2014. "Cloud Computing; Benefits, Risks and Recommendations for Information Security." 2009 ed. http://www.cloudwatchhub.eu/cloud-computing-benefits-risks-and-recommendations-information-security

Ezell, B.C., S.P. Bennet, D. Von Winterfeldt, J. Sokolowski, and A.J. Collins. 2010. "Probabilistic Risk Analysis and Terrorism Risk." *Risk Analysis* 30, no. 4, pp. 575–89.

HEFDC. n.d. "Risk Management and Assurance Solutions." https://hefdcgroup.com/assurance/

ISACA. 2014. "COBIT 5: A Business Framework for the Governance and Management of Enterprise IT." http://www.isaca.org/cobit/pages/default.aspx

ISO/IEC 31010. 2014. "Risk Management-Risk Assessment Techniques" 2009 ed. https://global.ihs.com/doc_detail.cfm?item_s_key=00534547&rid=Z06

Kaplan, S. and B.J. Garrick. 1981. "On the Quantitative Definition of Risk." *Risk Analysis* 1, no. 1, pp. 11–27.

Khan, K., and Q. Malluhi. 2013. "Trust in Cloud Services: Providing More Controls to Clients." *IEEE Computer* 46, no. 7, pp. 94–96.

Li, W., and L. Ping. 2009. "Trust Model to Enhance Security and Interoperability of Cloud Environment." *Cloud Computing, Lecture Notes in Computer Science* 5931, pp. 69–79.

Marsh, S. 1994. *Formalising Trust as a Computational Concept* [doctoral dissertation]. Stirling, Scotland: University of Stirling.

Maximilien, M., and M.P. Singh. 2004. Toward Autonomic Web Services Trust and Selection. *Proceedings of the 2nd International Conference on Service Oriented Computing (ICSOC '04)*. New York, NY: ACM, pp. 212–21.

Osterwalder, D. 2001. "Trust through Evaluation and Certification." *Social Science Computer Review* 19, no. 1, pp. 32–46.

Paradesi, S., P. Doshi, and S. Swaika. 2009. "Integrating Behavioral Trust in Web Service Compositions." *Proceedings of the 2009 IEEE International Conference on Web Services,* July 6–10, pp. 453–60, Los Angeles, CA.

Pearson, S. 2012. "Privacy, Security and Trust in Cloud Computing." In *Privacy and Security for Cloud Computing, Computer Communications and Networks,* eds. S. Pearson and G. Yee. New York, NY: Springer-Verlag, pp. 3–42.

Rashidi, A., and N. Movahhedinia. 2012. "A Model for User Trust in Cloud Computing." *International Journal on Cloud Computing: Services and Architecture (IJCCSA)* 2, no. 2, pp. 1–8.

Rousseau, D., S. Sitkin, R. Burt, and C. Camerer. 1998. "Not So Different After All: A Cross-discipline View of Trust." *Academy of Management Review* 23, no. 3, pp. 393–404.

Ryan, K.L.K., P. Jagadpramana, M. Mowbray, S. Pearson, M. Kirchberg, Q. Liang, and B.S. Lee. 2011. TrustCloud: A Framework for Accountability and Trust in Cloud Computing. *Proceedings of the 2nd IEEE Cloud Forum for Practitioners (ICFP),* July 7–8, Washington, DC.

Singh, S., and C. Morley. 2009. Young Australians' Privacy, Security and Trust in Internet Banking. *Proceedings of the 21st Annual Conference of the Australian Computer Human Interaction Special Interest Group: Design: Open 24/7,* New York, NY.

Tran, W.X., and H. Tsuji. 2008. "QoS Based Ranking for Web Services: Fuzzy Approaches." In *Proceedings of the 2008 4th International Conference on Next Generation Web Services Practices (NWESP '08).* Washington, DC: IEEE Computer Society, pp. 77–82.

Vu, L.-H., M. Hauswirth, and K. Aberer. 2005. "QoS-based Service Selection and Ranking with Trust and Reputation Management." In *Proceedings of the 2005 Confederated International Conference on the Move to Meaningful Internet Systems (OTM'05).* Berlin, Germany: Springer-Verlag, pp. 466–83.

Wang, P., K.-M. Chao, C.-C. Lo, C.-L. Huang, and Y. Li. 2006. "A Fuzzy Model for Selection of QoS-aware Web Services." In *Proceedings of the IEEE International Conference on e-Business Engineering (ICEBE '06).* Washington, DC: IEEE Computer Society, pp. 585–93.

Wang, P., K.-M. Chao, C.-C. Lo, R. Farmer, and P.-T. Kuo. 2009. A Reputation-based Service Selection Scheme, E-business Engineering. *Proceedings of the 2009 IEEE International Conference on e-Business Engineering (ICEBE),* October 21–23, pp. 501–506, Macau, China.

Wang, Y., and K.-J. Lin. 2008. "Reputation-oriented Trustworthy Computing in E-commerce Environments." *Internet Computing* 12, no. 4, pp. 55–59.

Xu, Z., P. Martin, W. Powley, and F. Zulkernine. 2007. Reputation-enhanced QoS-based Web Services Discovery. *Proceedings of the IEEE International Conference on Web Services (ICWS 2007),* July 9–13, pp. 249–256, Salt Lake City, UT.

Yudistira, A., P. Giorgini, F. Massacci, and N. Zannone. 2007. From Trust to Dependability Through Risk Analysis. *Proceedings of the Second International Conference on Availability, Reliability and Security (ARES),* April 10–13, pp. 19–26, Vienna, Austria.

CHAPTER 9

MANAGING RISK
IN THE CLOUD

As a result of economies of scale, cloud suppliers can provide state-of-the-art cloud ecosystems that are resilient and protected—much more protected than the surroundings of customers that handle their strategies. It has the potential to help many associations significantly. In Chapter 3 (Cloud Security Baselines) we discussed the need for companies to gain visibility into a cloud hosting supplier's support, to create the essential trust and also to correctly weigh the advantages of embracing a cloud-based remedy to put away a cloud client's information. The sensitivity of this saved data has to be considered contrary to the safety and privacy risks incurred. For instance, the advantages of a cloud-based alternative would rely on the cloud version, kind of cloud support achieved, the kind of information involved, the machine's criticality/impact degree, the price economies, the service type, and also any related regulatory requirements.

There are various kinds of risk that associations will need to tackle: application management, investment, funding, legal accountability, security, inventory, supply chain, safety, and much more. Risk management could be regarded as a holistic action that's integrated into every part of the organization. Risk management actions could be grouped into three classes based on the degree to which they tackle the risk-related issues:

1. The company level
2. The data system level

Risk management has to be a cyclically implemented procedure comprising a set of coordinated actions for controlling and handling risks. This procedure targets the improvement of tactical and strategic security and involves the implementation of hazard assessment, the execution of hazard mitigation plan, and also the employment of risk management methods and processes for the constant observation of the safety condition of the data system. Within this phase, we concentrate on the grade 3 safety risk linked to the performance and application of cloud-based data systems. To prevent and mitigate any dangers, adverse activities, service disruptions, strikes, or compromises, associations will need to measure their residual risk beneath the brink of the acceptable amount of risk.

The data systems risk management (grade 3 hazard management) is directed by the risk choices at grade 1 and tier 2. Risk choices in tiers 2 and 1 affect the most significant choice of the company's systems according to their information sensitivity, the acceptable cloud structure, and their defenses and countermeasures (i.e., safety controls) in the information system level.

At a cloud ecosystem, the intricate relationships among cloud "actors," the performers' respective assignments, business procedures, along with their supporting information systems demand an incorporated, ecosystem-wide risk management frame (RMF) that addresses all of the cloud actors' needs. As with any information system, to get a cloud-based data system, cloud "actors" are responsible for assessing their acceptable risk, which is dependent on the threshold determined by their risk tolerance into the cloud ecosystem-wide continuing threat. To efficiently manage information security threat at the ecosystem level, the improvement of tactical and strategic security involves the implementation of a hazard assessment, the execution of a hazard mitigation plan, as well as the employment of risk management methods and processes for the constant observation of the safety condition of the data system.

Internally, every cloud actor should further assign duties to their senior leaders, leaders, and agents.

- Near real-time observation, recognition, and comprehension by every "cloud actors" of the data security dangers arising from the performance or usage of this data system leveraging the cloud ecosystem.
- Accountability from the "cloud actors" and around real-time data sharing of those cloud actors' events, threats, risk control choices, and alternatives.

Risk can be expressed as a function of the probability that an adverse reaction occurs, multiplied by the size of such an adverse reaction. In data security, chances are known as a function of the dangers to the machine, the vulnerabilities which may be exploited, as well as the consequences of these vulnerabilities being exploited. Thus, safety risk assessments concentrate on identifying where at the cloud ecosystem adverse events can occur.

The risk-based method of handling data systems is a holistic action that has to be completely integrated into every part of the business, from development to SDLC (System Development Life Cycle) procedures, to safety control allocation and constant observation. An RMF operates primarily in grade 3 in the hazard management hierarchy, but it could also have connections at grade 1 and tier 2. Some illustration interactions include supplying the danger executive with comments from continuous monitoring and from consent decisions; devoting the upgraded threat data to alerting officials and also to data system owners. A safety lifecycle strategy, specifying data system requirements is a vital part of a system improvement process and has to start in a system's initiation stage. Considering that the safety conditions are a subset of the general functional and nonfunctional requirements, safety requirements have to be incorporated in the SDLC concurrently with all the functional and nonfunctional requirements.

The safety requirements have to be defined, and alternatives should be investigated and engineered at the beginning of their system's development. Fixing security for a patch as well as the machine and architecting and implementing alternatives independent of the SDLC is a much harder procedure that could incur greater prices with a lesser potential to mitigate risk.

The practice of employing the RMF's six eloquent, risk-related measures must be implemented concurrently by selected individuals or classes within distinct organizational functions, as a portion of (or in parallel with) the SDLC procedure.

NIST SP 800-37 Rev. 1 (2010) provides comprehensive advice regarding safety categorization, safety control choice, safety management implementation, security management evaluation, data system authorization, and security management tracking. The document encourages the notion of near real-time hazard management and continuing information system authorization via the execution of robust continuous monitoring procedures.

Risk evaluation (examine cloud surroundings to identify possible vulnerabilities and openings): identify operational, functional, safety, and privacy demands. Then, supplement the baseline safety control set dependent on the organizational evaluation of danger and the states of the operational environment. Produce a plan for the constant monitoring of safety control effectiveness. Document all of the controls in the safety program and review and accept the safety program.

Risk therapy (layout mitigation policies and strategies):

- Implement the security controls and explain in what way the controls are used within the data system and its surroundings of functionality.
- Evaluate the safety controls with appropriate assessment procedures as recorded in the evaluation program. The evaluation determines

if the controls have been implemented correctly and if they're successful in creating the desired result.

• Authorize information system performance based on the ascertained risk caused by the performance of this data system and the conclusion that this threat is acceptable.

Risk management (hazard observation—surveying, reviewing occasions, differentiating coverage alterations): Monitor the safety controls in the information system on a continuous basis including checking control efficacy, documenting modifications to the system or its environment of functionality, conducting safety impact analyses of those modifications, and reporting the safety condition of the machine to specified organization officials.

The reader is invited to examine NIST SP 800-37 Rev. 1 (2010) that can be leveraged here to the present discussion of employing the RMF at a cloud ecosystem. It's crucial to be aware that while the NIST record addresses complex data systems composed of numerous subsystems operated by various entities, it doesn't address cloud-based data systems or another sort of systems which leverage utility-based resources. When orchestrating a cloud ecosystem to get a cloud-based data system, cloud users, as owners of the information linked to the system, stay responsible for procuring the machine and the information commensurate with the information density. On the other hand, the cloud customers' degree of management and guide management fluctuate based on the cloud installation version.

As mentioned previously, the RMF (Risk Management Framework) procedure recorded in NIST SP 800-37 Rev. 1 is related by a cloud actor to the layers of this operational stack which are under control. In a cloud ecosystem version, which can be orchestrated solely by the cloud user and the cloud supplier, the RMF as recorded in Table 9.1 is employed by the cloud supplier to the lower portion of this stack, which can be constructed as part of the support given.

Table 9.1. NIST SP 800-37 Rev. 1

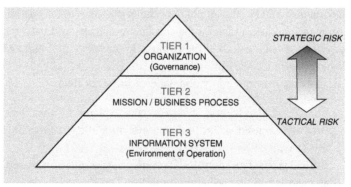

Cloud users will put on the RMF into the top operational layers, those assembled and deployed in addition to the cloud infrastructure provided as support. However, before obtaining cloud assistance, a cloud user should assess the risk associated with the adoption of a cloud-based alternative for a specific data system and program for the threat treatment and hazard control actions connected to the cloud-based operations of the system. To accomplish this, a cloud user should achieve the view of the full cloud ecosystem which will perform the operations of the cloud-based information platform.

Cloud users should also apply the RMF in a customized manner which allows them to:

- Carry out a hazard assessment
- Identify the best-fitting cloud structure
- Select the most acceptable cloud support
- Gain essential visibility to the cloud
- Define and negotiate essential hazard treatment and hazard control mitigations before delegating the SLA and moving with the safety authorization

Figure 9.1 depicts this RMF to your cloud ecosystem (RMF4CE) in the cloud customer's standpoint, demonstrating it as a repeatable process which encompasses the whole cloud ecosystem.

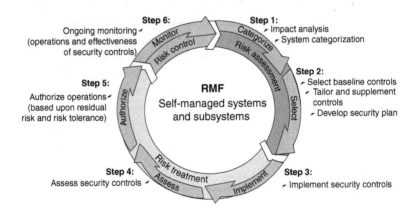

Figure 9.1. The RMF procedure recorded in Table 9.1 and NIST SP 800-37 Rev. 1

Cloud suppliers create cloud architectures and assemble cloud services which integrate core operation and operational characteristics, including privacy and security controls that meet baseline requirements. Their alternatives aim to fulfill the requirements of a massive pool of cloud customers as a means of minimum customization. A cloud supplier's choice and execution of its privacy and security controls relies in their effectiveness, efficacy, and limitations based on relevant laws, directives, policies, standards, or regulations where the cloud supplier has to comply with. The cloud customers' specific standards and mandates aren't understood and are projected as a standard core collection.

Cloud suppliers have considerable flexibility in determining what constitutes a cloud hosting support and consequently its associated border, but at the time that the machine is architected and implemented, they could presume the essence of information their cloud customers will create. Hence, the safety and privacy controls were chosen and executed utilizing a cloud supplier who fulfills the requirements of a high number of possible customers.

On the other hand, the concentrated nature of the cloud support enables a cloud supplier to engineer highly specific, technical security options that could offer a higher security position than in conventional IT systems. Implementing standardized or well-vetted methods to cloud support hazard management is essential to the achievement of the whole cloud ecosystem and its supported data systems. Considering that the cloud support is directly handled and regulated by the cloud supplier, employing RMF for this system doesn't require extra jobs beyond those of a classical IT system. Since a cloud supplier's reputation and business continuity are contingent on the smooth functioning and higher performance of the customers' options, when employing the RMF a cloud hosting supplier intends to compensate for potential weakness in their own cloud customers' solutions.

Broadly, organizations are more comfortable accepting danger when they have control over the procedures and equipment required. A high amount of control empowers organizations to weigh options, establish priorities, and act in their best interest when confronted with an event. For effective adoption of a cloud-based data system alternative, the cloud user has to be able to comprehend the cloud-specific qualities of the machine, the architectural elements for every service type and installation model, as well as the cloud actors' roles in creating a safe cloud ecosystem.

Moreover, it's also vital to cloud customers' company and mission-critical processes. They have the ability to:

- Ask the cloud suppliers—when applicable and through contractual means—about the agency arrangements and SLA in which the execution of privacy and security controls are in your cloud suppliers' duty.
- Evaluate the execution of stated privacy and security controls.
- Continuously track all identified safety and privacy controls. Considering the cloud customers are directly controlling and managing

the operational skills they execute, employing the RMF to those operational layers does not demand extra tasks or surgeries than is necessary with classical IT systems. With cloud-based solutions, a few subsystems or subsystem elements fall beyond the direct management of a cloud customer's organization.

Considering that the adoption of a cloud established alternative doesn't essentially provide for the same amount of safety and compliance with all the mandates from the traditional IT model, having the ability to execute a thorough risk assessment is essential to building trust from the cloud-based system since the very first step in simplifying its performance.

To maintain the safety level of their data system and information from a cloud-based alternative, cloud users require the capacity to spot most of the cloud-specific, risk-adjusted safety and privacy controls beforehand. They also need to ask from the cloud suppliers and agents, through contractual means and SLAs, if security and privacy elements are identified, and their controllers are entirely and correctly executed. Knowing the connections and interdependencies between the various cloud computing setup versions and support models is essential to understanding the safety risks involved with cloud computing. The differences between procedures and responsibilities for procuring different mixtures of support and installation models pose a substantial challenge for cloud customers. They will need to execute a comprehensive hazard assessment, to correctly recognize the safety and privacy controls essential to carry on the safety level of the surroundings as a portion of their risk treatment process, and also to track the operations and information after migrating to the cloud in reaction to their hazard control requirements.

Cloud users face many challenges when trying to ascertain which cloud support most effectively addresses their cloud computing requirement(s) while encouraging their enterprise and mission-critical procedures and solutions from the most secure and effective method. The target of this segment is to employ, by the cloud customer's standpoint, the RFM explained in this chapter and also to demystify to the cloud customers the practice of identifying, describing, categorizing, analyzing, and picking cloud-based solutions. Generally, a cloud customer embracing a cloud-based solution should follow the below measures:

1. Explain the service or program where a cloud-based alternative could be leveraged.
2. Identify all operational capabilities that have to be implemented with this service.
3. Describe the safety and privacy conditions and the safety controls required to secure the support or program.

For adopters of both NIST standards and guidelines, cloud users will need to ascertain the security group and related influence level of data systems according to Federal Information Processing. The data system's impact degree determines the safety control baseline that has to be implemented.

- Know the cloud suppliers' and agents' security position and inherited privacy and security controls.
- Tailor the safety and privacy controls to satisfy the safety and privacy requirements to the specific use case or identify additional compensating security controls, when required.
- Assign specific values to organization-defined safety parameters through explicit mission and choice statements.
- Supplement baselines with added privacy and security control enhancements, if necessary.
- Supply extra specification information to the execution of privacy and security controls.

Based upon the chosen cloud ecosystem structure, the company will keep and take upon itself the execution of the safety controls identified to the cloud user, augmented with all the additional pair of controls unique to the customer's case.

In Figure 9.2, we exemplify the RMF as applied to some cloud ecosystem in the cloud customer's perspective. The further measures that a cloud consumer should perform are put in italics. The RMF applied to the cloud ecosystem by the customer's view may be utilized to tackle the security risks connected with cloud-based data systems by integrating the results to the terms and conditions of the contracts with outside cloud

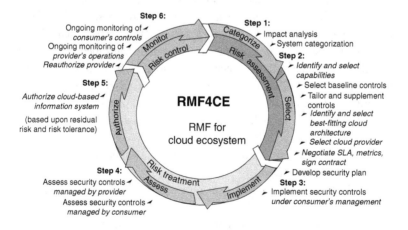

Figure 9.2. The RMF procedure recorded in Table 9.1 and NIST SP 800-37 Rev. 1

suppliers and cloud agents. Performance aspects of the terms and conditions can also be integrated into the SLA, which can be an integral part of the safety authorization procedure and of the support arrangement (SA) of the cloud customer, cloud supplier, an agent (when applicable). Contractual terms should contain guarantees of their cloud customer's convenient accessibility, or supplier's timely shipping, of cloud audit logs, constant observation logs, and some other user access logs.

The strategy covered by the measures in Table 9.2 empowers organizations to identify their conventional, hybrid vehicle, and system-specific safety controls and other safety conditions to procurement officials, cloud suppliers, carriers, and agents. A cloud consumer is responsible for performing a hazard assessment, identifying all of the security requirements due to their cloud-based support(s), and choosing the proper safety and privacy controls before picking a cloud supplier(s) and agent(s). Providers and agents which most fulfill the cloud customer's needs should be chosen either directly or by a repository of licensed cloud providers. The cloud user should execute a comprehensive evaluation, ideally with third-party independent assessors, to estimate the danger from using this service. Successful migration and creation into a secure cloud ecosystem rely on analyzing a cloud supplier's security position and system functionality, identifying remaining privacy and security controls that need to be implemented to guarantee the support or program, and identifying the cloud "actors" accountable for implementing those controls. The set of extra privacy and security controls has to be dealt with in arrangements involving the cloud user and other applicable cloud "actors."

The SLA is the part of this SA which details the amounts and kinds of providers to be supplied, such as but not restricted to the shipping period and performance parameters. Cloud suppliers utilize service-based agreements to spell out their offerings and conditions of support to possible cloud customers. The cloud customer should pay particular attention to the SLAs and require the business's procurement, technical, and policy specialists to make sure that the details of the SLA will permit the organization to satisfy its mission and functionality requirements. A challenge in selecting and comparing service supplies is that cloud suppliers may provide a default contract composed in the supplier's perspective. Such default contracts might not satisfactorily meet with the cloud customer's needs and might hamper the visibility of their cloud consumer to the delivery mechanisms.

In conclusion, embracing a cloud-based solution to an information system demands cloud customers to identify their safety condition, assess each potential service provider's privacy and security controls, negotiate SLAs and SAs, and build trust with all the cloud suppliers before

Table 9.2. Risk management framework—cloud consumer's perspective

Risk Management Activities	NIST SP 800-37 RMF Steps	Risk Management Framework—Cloud Consumer's Perspective
Risk assessment (analyze cloud environment to identify potential vulnerabilities and shortcomings)	1. Categorize	• Categorize the information system and the information processed, stored, and transmitted by that system based on a system impact analysis. Identify operational, performance, security, and privacy requirements
	2. Select (includes evaluate–select–negotiate)	• Identify and select functional capabilities for the entire information system, the associated baseline security controls based upon the system's impact level, the privacy controls, and the security control enhancements
		• Identify and select best-fitting cloud architecture for this information system
		• Evaluate/review cloud providers that meet consumers' criteria (architecture, functional capabilities, and controls)
		• Select cloud provider(s) that best meet(s) the desired architecture and the security requirements (ideally should select the provider that provides as many controls as possible to minimize the number of controls that will have to be tailored)
		• In the process, identify the controls that will be implemented by the consumer, the controls implemented by the provider as part of the offering, and the controls that need to be tailored (via compensating controls and/or parameter selection)
		• Negotiate SLA, metrics, and sign SA as part of the procurement process
		• Document all the controls in the security plan. Review and approve the security plan

Risk treatment (design mitigation policies and plans)	3. Implement	• Authorize the cloud-based information system to operate
	4. Assess	• Assess the cloud provider's implementation of the tailored security and privacy controls
		• Assess the implementation of the security and privacy controls, and identify any inheritance and dependency relationships between the provider's controls and consumer's controls
	5. Authorize	• Authorize the cloud-based information system to operate
Risk control (risk monitoring—surveying, reviewing events, identifying policy adjustments)	6. Monitor	• Continuous/near real-time monitoring of operations and effectiveness of the security and privacy controls under consumer's management
		• Continuous/near real-time monitoring of cloud provider's operations related to the cloud-based information system and assess the systems' security posture
		• Reassess and reauthorize (periodic or ongoing) the cloud provider's service

authorizing the support. A comprehensive hazard analysis coupled with protected cloud ecosystem orchestration introduced in this publication, together with adequate advice on negotiating SLAs, is meant to help the cloud buyer in managing risk and making educated decisions in embracing cloud solutions.

REFERENCE

NIST. February 2010. "Guide for Applying the Risk Management Framework to Federal Information Systems: A Security Life Cycle Approach," Special Publication 800-37 (Revision 1).

CHAPTER 10

CLOUD SECURITY ACCESS CONTROL

Cloud security access control may be an overwhelming job. Having tens of thousands of consumers accessing systems from around the globe and with many distinct devices can demand a great deal of planning and thinking. The many layers of possible safety risks are also a ripe target for hackers. Big conglomerates all around the world host virtual servers. Employees and consumers are in one part of the Earth, but the systems are in a different location. Sometimes servers are moved from one datacenter to another depending upon the time of day or a rise in demand from another location; therefore, we have to fasten the "moving targets." Consider Netflix—a sexy film comes out, or even a new show is released, and they transfer that content into the nearest place to the clients watching it. In addition, there is also the notion of BYOT (bring your own technology) and hence the data security pro's job becomes a lot harder. Among the most effective ways to have a look at the safety controls is to examine the layers where difficulties could happen. Every segment of the system has challenges that have to be dealt with. Occasionally those struggles may be easy to deal with, but generally, a comprehensive examination will have to be undertaken to avoid unauthorized access.

The very first and most exposed coating is the device layer. As shown in Figure 10.1, to think about safety, we begin with the consumer and continue through every stage. The user coating is generally the primary user interface apparatus. Most often, a computer, a tablet computer, or a mobile phone is utilized to get into the cloud system. Each telephone seller might have their particular browser, which might or might not comply with the safety standards of your company. A browser which works well under a single make of phone might lead to security problems in another make. The programming layer comes next, and it requires a careful execution for precisely what the program is supposed to perform, but it also ought to

prevent things the app is not supposed to do. The next layer is the host operating system. There are only a few specialists producing operating systems compared to the number of developers. Ultimately, we'll analyze the
network hardware and infrastructure. As shown in Figure 10.1, layers of
safety begin with the consumer and finish with the community; all must be
considered. Simple Network Management Protocol (SNMP)–based management not just generates management options for applications, systems,
complicated devices, and environmental management systems. Douglas
Mauro and Kevin Schmidt wrote a tech's manual to SNMP in a publication
titled "Essential SNMP" and they also provide that using the benchmark
allows for observation of many different sorts of apparatus and the health
of your system. Some devices are designed to contain temperature information. Warnings can be automatic along with other equipment (think
buffs) that could be taught to turn on automatically.

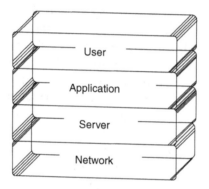

Figure 10.1. Layers of safety

Internet browsers dominate the consumer interface for many reasons.
The most straightforward reason is that the majority of users don't matter
what platform they're using. Telephones, tablet computers, notebooks, lap-
tops, and high-definition workstations have access to an Internet browser.
There are also a couple of web browsers that have variations for each of
the platforms.

Firefox and Chrome are just two that lead the marketplace (Net
Marketshare n.d.). The leading end for most cloud programs is your Internet browser. Connect into a browser-based application, and you're in
the cloud using the tools of a host in a data center somewhere on Earth.
Embedding safety at the front-end program rather than allowing different
applications to interfere with the relation between the host and the system gives a higher degree of protection than many web browser implementations. The safety bubble of the front end first assesses the internal

applications to ensure that the version of this front end is legitimate and not tampered with. This can occasionally cause an extended login interval for these kinds of devices. In case the front-end applications don't match the anticipated front-end version, the program denies access from that consumer.

Most commercial cloud applications and services need many users to combine their systems. This places much more challenges for the safety employee. For maintaining a protected internal system many businesses have limited access to additional programs. There are programs that may be set up on tablets and phones to restrict which programs a user can do. Just letting users perform requests using only your front end will assist in keeping out critical applications or invalid information requests from attacks. This becomes harder when an employee is permitted to bring their own device. If a person accesses cloud tools, administrators would like to understand who they are and restrict the user capability. There are many malware and viruses; the ability to have a front end that functions as a firewall against intrusion is vital. The leading end check is essential to securing the cloud and network servers before somebody gets in.

When creating applications to run in the cloud, applications engineers have lots of programming languages to pick from. Programming languages of reduced complexity are preferred by many, on account of their capacity to utilize computer hardware and their high-speed processing. Because of advancement in chip capabilities in the previous 10 years, higher level languages like Java and Ruby are increasingly being more popular for applications development. Preventing the software layer is quite complicated. The developer should avoid overflows of the stack, await code identification, and think about all of the probable things an individual or application on the consumers' computer may be capable of accomplishing. The developer has to be aware of the abuse of the enabled access and prevent unauthorized access of information. Applications have to be made to check for invalid requests in addition to ones that are valid. Preventing authorized users from doing illegal activities must forever be in the minds of the developer.

One technique used by program developers would be to trap errors and merely send back a generic message to the consumer when unauthorized tables or requests are being queried. Rather than returning the code and developer error message, the user gets a general warning they have done something wrong. Maintaining detailed error message from the consumer can keep particulars of this machine from reaching the user. Then they can start looking for vulnerabilities to this release and system. In the event the application programmer retains that data from the user, their application is a lot safer. A different way to secure your program is to produce tiers.

In Figure 10.2, the three-tier structure communicates via a center application ensuring greater protection to your database, revealing how information flows through the intermediary or middleware to be able to insulate the database. The three-tier structure was developed by a company named Open Environment Corporation, which was purchased by Borland in 1996. This system examines the program from three distinct tiers. The center bit of software understands the right format, design, business principles, and access control necessary to pass along a trade to the backend server.

Front-end user interface

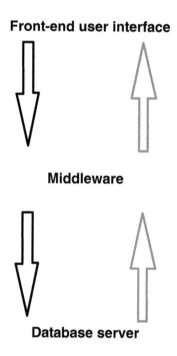

Middleware

Database server

Figure 10.2. The three-tier structure database structure

The backend database server only responds to requests in the middleware and just in the appropriate format with the right credentials. Any similarity in the petition in the middleware and the database returns nothing. This sort of programming necessitates layers of hardware to coincide with the three tiers. Together with the decreased prices for virtual servers, including many segments of equipment has become increasingly more commonplace. It raises the points of collapse; therefore, most program development businesses don't wish too many layers, but in the event the app is written appropriately, creating several instances of this middleware may result in improved reaction times of this machine. Just take an example where every server may handle 200 users.

Whenever your community develops beyond 200, including a different front-end host to the system would make sense, rather than adding more memory or processing power to a single server. Employing the three-tier architecture also produces the capacity to separate functions access for the developers. You might have six programmers working on a job. Having them specify and create the principles and the way the interfaces will operate provides them with the physical separation to deal with their portion of their undertaking. One advantage of the three-tier structure is that it insulates the database by the users. This is particularly true when your best aim is to maintain a secure database.

The majority of the World Wide Web is run on Linux and all its "tastes", as well as the Microsoft Windows host and all its variations. The program development platform selected by the project manager, developer, and administrator will frequently force the collection of the server operating system. There are numerous essential facets of server operating systems that need to be taken into consideration when deciding application development.

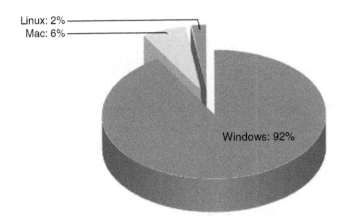

Figure 10.3. Shows a few of the most popular server operating systems such as Windows and Linux

The costes of the hosting and software could be a problem. Figure 10.3 shows a few of the most popular server operating systems such as Windows and Linux. When choosing a server seller, a whole slew of queries must be addressed, not the least of which is that there is access to an own server and the hardware that'll be operating it. Routine upkeep of your host is also critical. Security upgrades are significant to keep up with in your server platform, so inquire who is performing the software upgrades. Besides applications, hardware maintenance is done to keep the machine operating for a longer and healthier life. Disk drives can fail and have to be replaced. Besides care, there are lots of server tracking software that may warn you of issues with your host. These vary from assessing disc space to high memory usage. In fact, if the system is in use, and there's unusually large network traffic, a number of the host monitors will create an error. More particular monitors can reveal the information coming from any particular machine.

An alarm can be generated in the host administrators, or the device may take immediate corrective actions to obstruct the place that's causing the warning. Among the very best tactics to maintain the operating system procured would be to restrict physical access to the host to some few individuals. Most hosting facilities have a track log report of every individual entering and departing.

- Windows
- Linux
- VMWare
- Microsoft Azure
- OpenVMS
- OS/390
- Solaris
- macOS

There's also a significant push for some biometric accessibility. Some server rooms utilize hand geometry while some others utilize fingerprint technologies. Each biometric has its weaknesses and strengths, and the simple point is to assess what your seller is using and determine if this is sufficient for your program. Utilizing encryption, long, complicated passwords, customized user IDs that monitor the accessibility as well as the upgrades every administrator makes permits to get a fantastic audit trail. Understanding when programs are brought down and up and if applications are installed are also central monitoring that needs to be done to ensure administrators are following the principles.

Selecting infrastructure hardware is essential. The physical safety of your systems is critical for keeping out undesirable hackers and users. With physical access, someone can pull power cords and network strings, place in principle drives, reboot servers into a thumb drive, or slip the entire server. Many hosting companies have secure doors on server racks in addition to security measures to monitor and allow authorized personnel to the computer area. Most data center facilities have 24-hour video surveillance too.

In Figure 10.4, cloud computing sophistication and accessibility points provide you with a glimpse of the targets on your system. Along with procuring the host hardware, the system hardware also needs to be

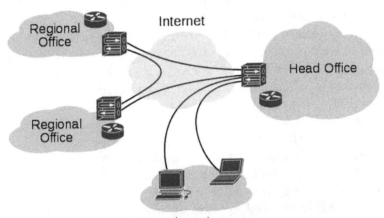

Figure 10.4. Cloud computing sophistication and accessibility points

secured. A secured computer room or telephone cupboard has become the most frequent approach to guarantee the system hardware. When an intruder or hacker has physical access to the system, they could install devices that can catch the information being transmitted. Great physical safety is merely the beginning. The next part to community security is actively managing the apparatus and allowing requests only from reliable devices. This can be accomplished via the usage of programs and physical Media Access Control (MAC) addresses in the community cards. Actively managed switches enable every interface to be assigned to a MAC address, so when another device connects to the change, it won't permit entry to the computer system. Many businesses will have many network connections in a workplace. Each ought to be handled and just physically linked to the change if it's in use.

Developing a physical barrier in the system is just about the safest way to stop unwanted interlopers. The next element is protecting the community from online intruders. Using network address translation (NAT) and also suitable firewall configurations can restrict the dangers from external hackers. Additionally, it is possible to limit which portions of the world are allowed to your hosted option. This makes harder once you have users that travel and are expected to look at their e-mail or Internet systems, but it's an alternative for the large security-conscious businesses. There are solutions you can buy in your firewall to block unique sites such as social websites. These kinds of providers could also be obstructed. Many firewalls have cubes for X-rated material. Some will block stock trading business and banking sites so that nobody has access to commercial websites from their network. Consequently, if somebody gains unauthorized access, they still won't be able to access financial institutions.

Your customers could maliciously become infected with a virus that turns their computer into a robot for a different user. These BOTs can subsequently be used by hackers to monitor what you're doing and let malicious code to go from the internal system. The real key to protecting from the inside is to get great spyware and antivirus practices. Additionally, updating your working and application software with the latest patches is crucial. Moreover, it contains routers and switches, which many IT people cannot perform at fixed intervals. A 6-month inspection of infrastructure ought to be done to create a report that confirms gear is up-to-date and functioning correctly. A new kind of virus was made and deployed across the Web in 2013. Often referred to as ransomware, the app would encrypt all your photos or all your files. A warning screen would appear and ask that you pay via bitcoin or other money trade like Western Union, or your documents would not be recoverable. Ransomware remained widespread till 2015 and will most likely be with us for a lengthy time. It's a challenging kind of virus to obstruct since users have access to their documents and an increasing number of folks are using encryption. The distinction is that the "keys" are at the user's hands rather than the criminals.

10.1. IMPROVEMENTS

There are just a few drawbacks to this cloud. Among the greatest is that you eliminate control over the physical hardware that's running your operation. Should you use Gmail from Google, then you're already outsourcing your e-mail to the cloud and then actually don't have any idea where all your information has been saved. Additionally, with all the free providers, the supplier is becoming something, right? The supplier gets to read and decode all your e-mails and images to be able to promote you better. Folks are paying Google to run advertisements which will target exactly what you would like and where you would like it. Another danger of this cloud is in case the service supplier goes bankrupt. Where does this leave you and your information? Make sure all your cloud info is backed up to another vendor's support or your local backup drive. There are some fantastic solutions which will make it possible for you to do so in several scenarios. The cloud is quite lively in regard to how it functions. Not only will companies have smaller IT departments, but they'll also have the less real onsite hardware. No requirement for a computer room except to command the system and connect to the cloud. "For both small and midsize businesses, the ability to outsource IT applications and services not only gives the capability to reduce overall costs but can also reduce the barriers to entry for several processing-intensive activities, because it removes the requirement for upfront funding investment and the requirement of keeping dedicated infrastructure" (International Telecommunications Union 2009). The cloud allows for outsourcing neighborhood servers and workstations to more efficient digital computers.

The cloud, being hosted on highest safety information centers, coupled with 256-bit encryption calculations, is among if not the very protected alternatives to store info. Nations such as China or India, unlike the United States, don't have a vast IT infrastructure. The cloud could open new markets and alternatives to international users permitting it to be valuable and innovative for people around the world. Cloud computing can decrease the cost of IT and also make quick expansion or contraction not as painful. Also, it is going to interconnect people in a way never seen or imagined before.

10.2. MULTILEVEL AUTHENTICATION

There are lots of multilevel authentication an administrator may use to stop unwanted access to sensitive cloud information. At this time, there's a big range in authentication criteria to get into any cloud-based server. Some have images that come together with your password, as another confirmation. You want to be aware of the text and also the picture that's related to your account. A remedy for this problem is to employ multilevel authentication utilizing three or more layers of complicated passwords. The second degree of authentication is a group degree password.

For some programs, there's a general password to enter a system; however, to make adjustments or overwrite current information another password is demanded. This sort of management degree authentication is observed in retail. A clerk may create a new trade but isn't able to clear a product or provide a refund with no supervisor level password.

10.3. ENCRYPTION

When a user uses one machine to get the cloud, then the keys for end-to-end encryption could be stored using an application on that device. Together with users able to get the cloud on multiple devices such as smartphones and tablets, it may be difficult to talk about these keys safely between devices. AES-256 is suggested for end-to-end. Encryption keys must be controlled and preserved by the end user. The domain manager (DM) handles domain preventing access to unregistered users before they get in the computer system. The customer side will encrypt the data and send it into the domain name, eliminating the direct connection from users from the cloud into the domain name. This may be referred to as border security, and there are lots of sellers to help protect your IT assets. Check Point Software Technologies Ltd. is a huge seller that addresses the challenges of system safety through firewalls and hazard prevention program.

10.4. PASSWORD ADMINISTRATION

There are various ways a user may use password management to their benefit in the cloud. These programs also provide robust encryption algorithms that can encrypt around 256 bits. The great thing about the cloud is that the capability to recoup passwords is remote anywhere on the planet.

Password management applications can have drawbacks though. The remedy for this is to sponsor the password supervisors in the cloud using the same online encryption criteria. The secret is to get a fantastic password and thwart any burglar at the door. Another choice is to utilize the changing tokens which have semi-passwords from the consumer and the remainder of it a random number generated on the symbol. The symbol is usually the size of a tiny USB drive. Along with this physical token, they also possess a software token which could run on your smartphone. The benefit is you don't have to take an excess device around.

10.5. DISTRIBUTED SERVERS

As time goes on, large site service providers like Google, Microsoft, and Amazon have changed from dispersed server facilities to enormous, sprawling data centers. The allure of this cloud-hosted data centers has enabled businesses and ordinary users to conserve time and money. Distributed cloud servers allow remote access to information anywhere in the world through an online connection. Whether the hosting business is large or small, the safety needs of your company ought to be fulfilled. One important thing to consider when deciding on a hosting firm is if you're sharing resources with a different site, obtaining a virtual server on a PC, or obtaining a whole server for your applications. When considering safety, having your hardware is most likely the safest. Unfortunately, most firms don't wish to invest $500 or more to get a dedicated host. A digital machine may provide you excellent security while still maintaining excellent cost controls. To get a public facing site with static info or hyperlinks to your social websites, a shared host operating WordPress ought to be safe enough.

Many systems only demand a simple user-generated password to obtain access, while some are somewhat more robust. Consider the demands of your program, what laws regarding data breaches might be appropriate for you, and attempt to mitigate your risk through proper security methods. SNMP, encryption, antivirus, and strong passwords are required to track and protect almost any cloud system from assault efficiently. Individual negligence of safety is arguably the most significant contributor to both network and cloud invasion. Inadequate password choice, stolen notebooks, sharing the same password among different sites, and making computers unlocked for simple access for real usage are all top dangers.

REFERENCES

International Telecommunications Union. 2009. "Distributed Computing: Utilities, Grids & Clouds." ITU-T Technology Watch Report 9.
Net Marketshare. n.d. "Desktop Browser Market Share," SM-Net Applications .com https://www.netmarketshare.com/browser-marketshare.aspx
SNMP. n.d. "Secure Internet Management and SNMP." http://www.snmp.com

CHAPTER 11

CLOUD SECURITY RISK MANAGEMENT

Cloud security risk management is an often discussed and analyzed topic that, in the past few decades, has caught the interest of many professionals and scholars. It reunites distinct remarkable elements under one group: the technical and financial relevance of cloud systems, whose diffusion has been one of the most notable phenomena of the previous decade. The growing concerns about information security include privacy; the increasing relevance of risk management and analysis applied to information technology; and systems as procedures that encompass technical aspects in addition to compliance, governance, and company. However, cloud security risk management for a research area and a set of methodologies, analyses, and techniques is still far from being a mature subject.

On the contrary, it is riddled with uncertainty derived from the early phases of security risk analysis, mainly employed to cloud systems, and also the relatively poor expertise in handling the dangers of cloud. For these reasons, there is still ongoing debate about which risks should be considered cloud-specific and new, which established risk-mitigating solutions and criteria could be applied to the cloud environment, and so on. In this chapter, we survey the fundamental facets of cloud safety risk management, starting with the definition of danger and moving to an investigation of cloud-specific dangers. Concerning risk management, we highlight the contractual nature of cloud computing, thus focusing specifically on service level agreements (SLAs), an issue that has become the topic of numerous relevant analyses and proposals in the past couple of decades.

11.1. RISK IN THE CLOUD

In the process of managing risks in the cloud, an individual could easily argue by asking what a threat is, signifying an excessive diversion into the history of risk analysis. Everybody appears to understand what risk is; we continuously have to recognize dangers and manage them to suffer the consequences when we fail. When we drive a car, take medicines, decide on vacation, make choices for our career, select a financial investment, and romance or marry our cherished one, we recognize the dangers and manage them. It's a fact of life—we all know what a risk is and also teach it to our kids as part of traditional parental instruction.

Perhaps, we could even say that with no dangers, life could be tremendously dull and pointless. Why are you currently stressing what risk is rather than focusing immediately on recent improvements of this cloud and risk? Why don't you skip these fundamentals and talk about the cloud with those fantastic chances for perimeterless networked associations and still mysterious dangers?

Why resuming decade-old discussions from risk analyses or game concept rather than presenting fancy cryptography and international laws as well as sketching plots of impending hacker attacks and catastrophic power outages?

We are doing so because it could be too risky an assumption to deem the concept of risk as unambiguous. It could be a more serious mistake than that: it is a fact that the idea of risk isn't unambiguously given, perhaps not widely shared, and, most important of all, extremely context dependent. In short, whenever we try to explain what risk is, we always struggled to find a vague general description and we turn to anecdotes and illustrations taken from our experiences. The same is followed in the literature. Risk is defined in a variety of ways, often mutually irreconcilable—we could discover different definitions of risk among international criteria—and it is often oversimplified to acquire a suitable operational definition as a handy formula, and also the essential character of risk is neglected. There is no risk without doubt and uncertainty is irreducible when dealing with risks. This is not meant to say that doubt and then risk can't be mitigated or managed; it could, apparently, but it couldn't be eliminated from dangerous scenarios whatever technology, management method, or control is used.

In the field of risk analysis, many writers have made a distinction between uncertainty and risk (e.g., Knightian doubt) (Knight 1921, 2012). On the one hand, that distinction has not been adopted uniformly or by the majority of scholars. On the other hand, it's not particularly relevant for the present chapter, and much worse, framing both concepts as mutually distinct instead of strictly correlated may lead to ambiguity. Therefore, let us believe that risk is intrinsically tied with uncertainty: dealing with risk means being able to deal with uncertainty, possibly many sorts of doubt, not just uncertainty about probabilities (or chance) associated with different outcomes.

We might doubt the motivation of a decision maker or their cognitive biases. We may also have to think about who the decision makers are, more generally, who are those able to affect a decision. This is especially common, for example, in change management: who are those able to determine, even partly, the results of a technological shift in a company?

Also, then, what is the danger of failure due to the misalignment of objectives between the board and the employees or between the headquarters and one or more branches? Further, we also have uncertainty about the efficacy of many technologies; this is particularly insidious when the efficacy is incrementally quantifiable, like for data security.

11.2. INDIRECT MEASUREMENTS AND METRICS

Indirect measurements and the absence of clear metrics are problems very near to the subject of this chapter. As reported by interviews and surveys with IT professionals and CIOs, data security risks are considered to be one of the most crucial for cloud computing.

The fact that security is a top concern for networked systems as well as Internet-based solutions is not a surprise, naturally. However, considering the risks of cloud computing, it tells us that we will have difficulty in finding demonstrably effective strategies to estimate those risks quantitatively, provided there is difficulty in getting direct measures of safety. In fact, the majority of the risk analysis and management approaches employed in data security are qualitative by nature, which makes them a lot easier to handle but also, occasionally, somewhat simplistic. Again, doubt is popping up; the methods implemented to take measures of safety are uncertain or have uncertain effectiveness. The more they aim at producing a precise hazard estimate, like value in a structured rank or a matrix, the higher the danger that the risk assessment is grossly miscalculated (frequently, there's also a recursive impact in risk analysis to contemplate). In the long run, it is an issue of handling an operational risk (i.e., the residual risk after the chosen mitigation alternatives are applied).

In controlled situations, either by legislation or by contractual obligations, it is sometimes simplistically assumed that the presence of laws or contractual obligations is sufficient to get rid of uncertainty: "At least, there's a contract with composed clauses and obligations" is your ultimate conclusion that some assume, to prevent complexity. Regrettably, in the real world, nothing is so simple when legal disputes arise. It depends upon wordings and on fine details; it mostly depends on what was not written in the arrangement than on what has been written. The outcome of a legal dispute over the terms of a contract could be very uncertain, and it is meat for attorneys rather than for technologists. Here again, uncertainty arises and consequently dangers in a scenario where specific electronic services are provided according to a commercial contract, and thus the resolution of disputes is a more valid concern than a specialized one.

One fundamental problem is represented by SLAs, the means to govern a cloud computing relationship between two parties. However, as for legislation and industrial contracts, only saying that some SLAs will be stipulated does not resolve risk and uncertainty, since it depends on what those SLAs define or leave. Then there are industrial sources of uncertainty and risks. Many are well understood because they're the same for traditional corporate systems, hence not specific to cloud computing. Internet-based applications and web technologies are notable examples. Then there are sources of uncertainty and hazard specific to cloud computing, but as we will discuss next, experts and scholars are still fighting for the identification of these specific cloud computing dangers. There is no broad consensus; you will find studies pointing to some risks and others confusing about the specificity of those risks. The exact definition of specific cloud computing dangers is still mainly an open problem, possibly requiring new options and original approaches, and is among the most debated research areas.

11.3. DEFINITIONS OF RISK

The definition of hazard may be opportunistically given because it fits according to one's goals. For instance, if the goal is to examine the effects of volatility and uncertainty, risk is often defined irrespective of the sign of the result (i.e., gain or loss); when the situation is indeed a zero-sum game a particular risky prospect might be a loss for some parties and a gain for others. Finance is mentioned in this circumstance. In other contexts, instead, scholars and analysts have indicated a difference between dangers and chances, the former indicating adverse outcomes or losses, the latter favorable outcomes or profits.

It's the standard of computer engineering and data security to refer to dangers as strictly adverse uncertain outcomes, such as system failures, disconnections, malfunctioning, programming mistakes, hacker attacks, or sabotage. Traditional models of decision under risk, for example, Von Neumann and Morgenstern's Model of Expected Utility (Von Neumann and Morgenstern 2007), in the 1940s, didn't consider losses or adverse outcomes, given that they leave the party in charge of a decision worse off than merely doing nothing.

More recently and more specifically to information technology, we can find relevant examples of different definitions of danger in widely known and implemented standards like the ones published from International Organization for Standardization (ISO)/International Electrotechnical Commission (IEC) and the U.S. National Institute of Standards and Technology (NIST). The NIST Special Publication 800-39 Handling Information Security Risk Organization, Mission, and Information System View of 2011 defines risk as: "A measure of the degree to which a potential circumstance or occasion jeopardize an entity, and typically a function of (i) the adverse impacts that could arise whether the event or event happens; and (ii) that the likelihood of occurrence" (NIST 2011). In both criteria there's the definition of information security risk as: "The risk to organizational processes (including mission, functions, image, reputation), organizational resources, individuals, other organizations, and the Country due to the possibility of unauthorized access, use, disclosure, disruption, modification, or destruction of information and/or information systems."

It's intriguing to consider how those definitions changed in 10 years. The definition of information security risk was not given in 2002.

Even with this type of fast syntactical analysis, we can see that in 10 years the definition of risk within an IT context evolved to be elaborated, but its right formula remained precisely the same, being the danger of the product of a probability/likelihood of an occasion and the adverse effect of the event. As we'll see, this definition (in short, hazard = likelihood $\times$ effect) is usually adopted in almost all IT-related evaluations, essays, and research articles, although both in real projects and in different disciplines and industrial fields the analytical definition of risk is often distinct, such as more parameters or even much more complex functional relations. Proposed frameworks for quantitative risk assessment of cloud security like QUIRC are also dependent on the same basic definition of risk as the combination of a likelihood and an impact (Saripalli and Walters 2010). The ISO/IEC world isn't qualitatively different from the NIST situation: the definition of risk evolved throughout the years and, in some cases, took divergent paths.

Let's consider first the ISO/IEC 27001 Information Security Management standard in the initial 2005 version and the revision of 2013. To the contrary, ISO/IEC 27001:2013 describes the ISO/IEC 27000:2009 (ISO/IEC 2009), which officially set the vocabulary for the whole 27000 families of ISO standards. There, hazard is defined as the "combination of the likelihood of an event and its outcome," which is a simpler and easier definition than the NIST one, although qualitatively it's still hazard = likelihood $\times$ effect (supposing the simplistic equivalence between

chance and likelihood). The ISO/IEC 27001:2013 expressly refers to "dangers and chances"; therefore, we can deduce that danger applies to negative impacts only.

This standard isn't specifically tailored to information technology, but this International Standard plans to harmonise risk management procedures in the present and future standards. It provides a common approach in service of standards by managing specific risks and industries, and does not replace these standards (Brender and Markov 2013).

Thus, the ISO 31000 standard should be considered as a benchmark for another risk-related ISO standards. Below is the first paragraph of this introduction:

> Organizations of all sizes and types confront external and internal factors and influences which make it unclear if and when they will achieve their aims. The effect that this uncertainty has on a company's objectives is "risk."

Notably, risk here is "the impact of doubt" on goals, which can be an entirely different definition from all of the previous ones, much more in line with researches and studies out of the IT area, focusing on the incidence of doubt and its influence instead of providing an operational, rudimentary formula where the uncertainty is buried into just the probability/likelihood of an adverse event. These are only some examples, though remarkable, of the heterogeneity of definitions and concepts that we ought to expect to find when dealing with the notion of danger. The Open Group nicely describes another difference in meaning and language when risk is referred to by considering how different specializations have developed their view of danger:

> This gap is especially evident between company managers and their IT risk/security specialists/analysts. For example, business managers discuss the impact of reduction not regarding how many servers or operational IT systems will stop to provide normal service, but rather what will be the impact of losing these common services on the company's capability to continue to trade generally, quantified regarding value. The effect is a failure to satisfy applicable regulatory requirements that could induce them to limit or perhaps cease trading and perhaps become liable to heavy legal penalties. (The Open Group 2009)

Such differences are especially important to consider since IT usually risks an issue for both technologists and supervisors, and the two categories

of professionals must socialize with each other (e.g., technologists providing technical analyses for supervisors and supervisors defining strategies or company priorities for technologists). Therefore, still mentioning The Open Group (2009) essay,

> "(. . .) [if] a business manager will consider a threat as something which could bring about a loss which the business cannot absorb without seriously damaging its trading position", and a technologist rather thinks of it as "Anything that's capable of behaving in a way leading to harm to an advantage or organization; for example, acts of God (weather, geological events, etc.); malicious actors; errors; failures"

then we ought to be aware that there's ample room for misunderstandings in the communication between the two categories.

11.4. RISK AND CLOUD

The prior segments, although not directly associated with cloud computing, were needed to frame the context of the discussion of risk in utilizing the cloud: the multifaceted character of language and uncertainty depends on specialization.

Concerning cloud computing, likely the central question related to hazard is, are risk or hazard aspects peculiar to cloud computing systems and, thus, do they require new analyses and alternatives for conventional ones designed for networked, dispersed information systems?

The response that the literature is telling us is not universal; it isn't recognized whether cloud computing is introducing new IT risks and what they are. A lot has been written in the last 10 years on cloud computing and security, but the definition of cloud-specific dangers is an open issue. We will outline the state-of-the-art work of current research and debate.

11.4.1. SECURITY RISKS NOT PARTICULAR TO CLOUD COMPUTING

Yanpei, Paxson, and Katz in 2010, analyzing security problems affecting cloud computing environments, titled their work "What is new about cloud computing protection?", signaling that the response was not trivial, in which probability there was a certain level of overhype in regular announcements of new security threats brought by cloud computing.

Instead, as declared by the authors: "We argue that few cloud computing security issues are fundamentally new or intractable; often what appears 'new' is indeed only relative to 'conventional' computing of the past several decades." Therefore, assessing security and also risk issues of cloud computing, the initial effort should be devoted to excluding issues that aren't specific to cloud computing and for which alternatives or countermeasures are already known and accessible. "Do not reinvent the wheel" is a rule of thumb in these scenarios. Let us believe the NIST definition of cloud computing (Mell and Grance 2011), which is among the most cited:

> Cloud computing is a model for enabling ubiquitous, convenient, on-demand network access to a shared pool of configurable computing tools (e.g., networks, servers and storage, software, and services) that can be rapidly provisioned and introduced with minimal direction effort or service provider interaction.

Such a model, concerning clients, is almost always implemented via a web-based remote configuration port.

The installation could suffer from conventional problems related to web applications, remote communications, and misconfigurations (by mistake or purposeful). Incidents may happen (and did occur), but from the analysis, the causes should not be associated with cloud computing. As an example, a reduction of confidentiality on the communication channel may happen from a vulnerability in an encryption library, but that is neither a "cloud computing vulnerability" nor a "cloud computing threat." It is a vulnerability/risk of remote communication using such a library.

This version, in regard to customers, is nearly always implemented through a web-based remote configuration port. The installation could undoubtedly suffer from traditional problems associated with web applications, remote communications, and misconfigurations (by error or purposeful). Incidents may occur (and did indeed happen), but from the analysis, the causes shouldn't be related to cloud computing. As an example, a reduction of confidentiality on the communication channel may occur from a vulnerability in an encryption library, but this is neither a "cloud computing vulnerability" nor a "cloud computing threat." It is a vulnerability/risk of all remote communication using such library.

Many other similar cases can be identified; however, the important message here is not to tag old issues as fresh, since already recognized solutions are extremely likely to become accurate, efficient, cheaper than creating new ones from scratch. Considering the cloud provider, many issues that may arise will be the same of all data-hosting setups. Data inconsistency, copies, network failures, blackouts, and errors by system administrators, in addition to common security threats of networked associations, aren't cloud-specific generally. Regrettably, many analyses, both academic and industrial, don't make this kind of attempt at clarification and contemplate too many safety risks as cloud-specific (Carlson 2014; Carroll, Van Der Merwe, and Kotze 2011; Janeczko 2011; Rong, Nguyen, and Gilje Jaatun 2013). As an example, they affirm that if a vulnerability is widespread in state-of-the-art cloud hosting, it has to be considered cloud-specific.

Along with that line of reasoning, the logical consequence is to incorporate under the label of cloud-specific an inordinate amount of vulnerabilities not specific to cloud, but specific to the underlying technology. This way, the threat will be to confound analysts and professionals by overlapping web applications to cloud computing, the former being a pair of technology, the latter a model for service provision that's implemented by means of traditional and innovative technologies (such as inheriting both their strengths and flaws) and providing enhanced benefits and maybe introducing new vulnerabilities. Thus, as we do not recognize cloud computing benefits with those of generic web applications, but worry about particular novelties, in precisely the same vein we ought to label as cloud-specific only peculiar vulnerabilities.

11.4.2. CLOUD-SPECIFIC HAZARDS

The request for in-depth analyses of cloud-specific dangers and safety vulnerabilities has inhabited IT, analysts, because the start of the cloud computing age in the last 10 years, and remains today. Cloud rewards for businesses are promoted aggressively, while free solutions, formerly not known as cloud-based (e.g., free e-mail services), have attained tremendous success among the consumers. Let's begin with a few of the most cited and influential investigations up to now about cloud computing threat: the 2009 report from the European Union Agency for Network and Information Security (ENISA), the European Union service for the community and data security. The report isn't recent—6 years has been a considerable period for advanced IT providers—and read now it indeed reveals the absence of practical experience at the time of writing. Instead, the report relies on hypotheses attracted by a pool of specialists as well as the editors.

Precisely, they realized contractual and management issues as strikingly essential for cloud computing and also place considerable focus on them:

- Reduction of governance
- Compliance risk

- Data protection
- Insecure or imperfect information deletion
- Malicious insider

This listing combines user-side and provider-side dangers, but it's especially interesting because three from those five dangers aren't technical and largely based on contractual arrangements and governance of data methods (i.e., reduction of governance, lock-in, compliance), one is associated with the large redundancy and dynamical movement of information average of cloud computing systems (i.e., speculative or faulty data deletion), and others are mostly generic threats not really unique to computing. It's also interesting to check the record of less significant dangers mentioned by ENISA.

A number of them are not cloud-specific dangers, such as individuals from information in transit on the web or distributed denial of service (DDoS), but a few are cloud-specific. Reduction of company standing because of cotenant actions sounds embarrassing (i.e., why just reputation dangers from cotenants' action?), but gets the significant merit to stage to multitenancy as one primary source of cloud dangers; conflicts between client hardening processes and cloud surroundings are a bit too narrowly defined and hypothetical, but implicitly it highlights among the very most, if not the most, crucial cloud-specific threat: the potential mismatch between client's safety policies and also people of the cloud supplier and also the difficulty (or impossibility) to carry out an audit. That can be a particularly insidious threat as technical, governance, and financial facets are indicative and it proves extremely hard to examine, quantify, and somehow mitigate the dangers coming from this type of multifaceted nature.

The NIST's counterpart of this ENISA report was the 800-144 Guidelines on Practice and Security in Public Cloud Computing, printed in 2011. While exceptionally comprehensive and in several parts like the investigation done by ENISA, NIST was much less exact and categorical as ENISA to recognize cloud-specific dangers. The story is much more elaborate and many standard security problems are discussed, occasionally overlapping with other NIST publications. This is what NIST writers have said: "Public cloud suppliers' default offerings usually do not signify a particular organization's safety and privacy requirements," which is very similar to ENISA's conflicts between client hardening techniques and cloud environment. But, they continue:

Non-negotiable service arrangements where the conditions of service are prescribed entirely from the cloud supplier are usually the standard in people cloud computing. Negotiated service arrangements are also possible. [. . .] Critical information and software may need an agency to take on a negotiated service agreement to utilise a public cloud.

This is a critical point that today remains the subject of many reports and talks about cloud dangers and with no clear and functional answers.

On the one side, it's been recognized that standardized SLAs provided by cloud suppliers don't meet the demand for risk control of several clients and, moreover, don't include security level dimensions (Baset 2012; Petcu and Craciun 2014). On the flip side, cloud consumers, usually, don't have the negotiating capacity for imposing contractual conditions to economic behemoths such as cloud suppliers, which base their business model on rigorous service standardization to decrease management costs, greater automatization, and economies of scale. In this scenario lies the unresolved issue: SLA personalization on a per-client basis is equally necessary and impractical for handling cloud dangers.

Considering the paper "What's New Concerning Cloud Computing Security" (Yanpei, Paxson, and Katz 2010), it's the multitenancy feature and the company and technical problem of auditing that are recognized as the two most critical cloud-specific sources of danger.

The multitenancy feature might be accountable for a complete array of dangers, that is, brand new significance to your technicalities or fresh significance for effect size and the probability of the occasion.

Mutual auditability is the logical outcome of complex relationships between cloud celebrities concerning some standard support user/provider scenario.

We've already pointed to a few of the primary motives for this high sophistication, that is, the entangling of specialized, governance, and financial issues binding cloud customers and suppliers. Mutual auditability will be needed for quantifying support and safety levels, for more celebrated solving episodes and regaining processes, and it's a necessity for the definition of prolonged, scalable, and personalized SLAs. However, whereas in concept the advantage of mutual auditability was recognized, in practice, it never occurs that a cloud client could audit a cloud-hosting supplier, except in extraordinary circumstances. Theoharidou et al. (2013) recent analysis points to multinenancy as the primary source of cloud-specific threats. In their study, privacy dangers deriving from multitenancy happen to be analyzed. Compliance and liability are discovered to be extraordinarily tricky, again, because of the enormous complexity governing the connection between users and the supplier.

Another result was reached by Ryan (2013) in his investigation: "Consequently, the truly distinctive challenge posed by cloud computing protection boils down to only 1 thing: The information in the cloud could be retrieved from the cloud supplier." In his opinion, therefore, it's not multitenancy that's the real differentiating factor connected to known safety risks, but rather the transfer of management and control over assets and data from the proprietor to a supplier. Under this view, cloud suppliers can't be compared to easy data-hosting services, since the important feature isn't data storage (for that matter conventional encryption is the alternative for solitude); rather, cloud suppliers are needed to implement "nontrivial computations" that vary based on the sort of cloud support (i.e., support/platform/infrastructure for a support). Advanced cryptographic techniques such as protected multiparties computation (Bennani, Damiani, and Cimato 2010; Cramer, Damgård, and Nielsen 2001; López-Alt, Tromer, and Vaikuntanathan 2012) or utterly homomorphic encryption (Gentry 2009) are analyzed for cloud computing, although these are approaches that necessarily increase the complexity of the solution in a stage nevertheless tough to handle in creation to get large-scale cloud technologies. Then, the threat envisaged by Ryan of the way to ensure confidentiality by a cloud supplier must still rely upon contractual duties prohibiting a supplier from disclosing customer information, but there isn't any clear technical alternative that will be implemented in large industrial environments. A current study about citizenship danger in cloud processes is a first effort to supply a comprehensive functional solution, but it is still based on rigorous modeling assumptions and gaming case studies (Damiani, Cimato, and Gianini 2015). Claycomb and Nicoll (2012) of all CERT (Computer Emergency Response Team) noted instead the way the ordinary dangers posed by insiders have cloud-specific connotations worth profound evaluation. The apparent threat posed by insiders is that of a fictitious secretary of this cloud supplier, who might undoubtedly provoke every type of acute damage. On the other hand, the situation isn't fundamentally different from each data-hosting business and, based on CERT writers, we have very little evidence relating to this from information on events. The authors consider two additional cases instead, more tailored to some cloud situation: an insider exploiting cloud-specific vulnerabilities along with an insider employing a cloud system to undermine a few suppliers' local resources. In the first scenario, the privileged place of the insider could allow him/her to spot and exploit vulnerabilities in the cloud infrastructure to get access to sensitive data to market or use for private benefit. In the second instance, instead, an insider could utilize his/her place in the cloud tools for illegal purposes (e.g., starting a DDoS toward an outside goal) or to exfiltrate sensitive data (Moore et al. 2011).

Analyses that only relabeled conventional security dangers of Internet-based systems as cloud-specific are somewhat futile or even plainly misleading. As a result, the pursuit of a cloud-specific hazard assessment definition nevertheless represents for many professionals and scholars the most challenging problems in cloud computing research. Some recent works have concentrated on specific features of cloud hazard assessment and management that were overlooked before. Keller and König (2014) emphasized the inadequate understanding of their underlying system structure of a cloud supplier to be among the severe hurdles to the first identification of cloud-specific dangers.

A detailed Microsoft article (Stone and Noel n.d.), instead, presented a helpful evaluation of cloud hazard management over the proper framework of ISO 31000 (ISO/FDIS 2009), such as employing a renowned global standard instead of "reinventing the wheel" with another hazard process administration. Risk evaluation is split typically into three stages, namely, hazard identification, hazard analysis, and hazard evaluation followed closely by the direction stage of risk therapy. The overall ISO risk procedure is subsequently utilized to appraise a cloud-service alternative.

These are typical problems that contribute to change direction and hazard evaluation.

11.4.3. SAFETY SLA FOR CLOUD SERVICES

Moving risks to third parties was the basis of risk control for quite a very long time. It gave birth to the insurance company and to actuarial research utilized to assess insurance risks.

Generally, dangers are moved from one party to another by stipulating an official contract between the two. Cloud options and generally nearly all service/infrastructure externalizations possess precisely the very same attributes. Businesses often externalize solutions to cloud suppliers not only so that they could cover less (if it's the case), but also so that they be relieved of dangers related to handling an intricate technological infrastructure or support, such as dangers of network failures, network support, or electricity blackouts. Generally, cloud-based providers all mitigate these dangers, since it's the cloud supplier who faces the unwanted consequences (or the majority of these). The cloud client pays the standard fee. Sadly, this is merely the concept (or even the "advertising fact").

In training, as usual, things can certainly mess up, as who's in control of everything, and to that extent dangers are moved from a customer to a cloud supplier and strictly rely on contractual conditions specified within an SLA. Because of this, SLAs play such a crucial part in talks about cloud dangers: it's because frequently everything depends on these.

When cloud-specific dangers are believed, two issues involving SLAs will be the topics of ongoing research and debate among specialists: cloud SLA and safety SLA. The very first, cloud SLA, is supposed to recognize a cloud-specific SLA, which should provide explicit guarantees for average requirements of users and needs to be tailored for their particular requirements. The next, safety SLA, defines an SLA especially defined to ensure a specified security level. Finally, both kinds of SLAs must innovate at an ordinary cloud-oriented SLA definition using both particular provisions with a focus on safety, this being perceived as the primary supply of dangers to cloud systems. For clarity and to reflect the present state of the art, we maintain both cloud-oriented SLAs different in the current chapter.

A realistic presentation of the constraints of cloud SLAs was awarded by Baset (2012). Also, the SLAs of several cloud suppliers are examined about important parameters of the caliber of a cloud provider. Unsurprisingly, none has shown sufficient performance warranties, and all have put the burden of discovering SLA violations on clients.

- Service assurance: The metrics used to gauge the supply of this ceremony over a time interval (e.g., accessibility, response time)
- Service warranty time interval: The length over which an agency warranty ought to be fulfilled (e.g., a billing month, the term since the final claim, 1 hour)
- Service warranty granularity: The source scale to define a service warranty (e.g., per agency, per data center, per case, per trade)
- Service guarantee exception: Instances excluded from the test (e.g., misuse of this system by a client, downtime because of scheduled maintenance)
- Service charge: The sum credited to the client for assurance offenses (e.g., partial or complete refund of their client fee)
- Service breach coverage and measurement: How and when that reports and measures violations of an agency warranty

Merely considering this listing of overall elements, it needs to be clear how "the devil of cloud computing" can also be very likely to be located in the information. Simply trading a partial, rather than a full, refund to get a lesser service fee varies the risk profile of this SLA. More likely, however, given the extraordinary potential to get a client to pay back the contractual stipulations, and excluding system abuses in the warranties (as many current SLAs prescribe) renders the consumer unprotected from most safety risks.

The analysis (Baset 2012) believed a number of the very well-known cloud suppliers. All of these guarantee service accessibility, though even when a service ought to be regarded as "accessible," it's typically filled with contractual subtleties along with the origin of acute misalignments between the pursuits of a cloud client and people of a supplier. No safety or other rigorously cloud-specific attributes are believed explicitly; that is, safety as other facets could be regarded as guaranteed due to their effects on service accessibility, but it's a mostly insufficient type of security against safety risks. Other elements of a regular SLA can differ considerably between cloud suppliers.

The support granularity guarantee fluctuates from the information center to each case; it is not specified if scheduled maintenance is frequently excluded from measures of support accessibility; the length of scheduled maintenance, also, isn't always defined (unsurprisingly, when contemplated, since it might sensibly alter the bonded system availability rate); the support warranty period might differ from a complete year into a billing or a calendar month. For the support charge, SLAs have the best variability, which makes it extremely hard to compare one commercial supply to a different one and grasp how successful the threat transfer is by the consumer to the supplier. The refund is frequently a portion of the consumer invoice if a specific service accessibility threshold isn't fulfilled (e.g., 10 percent of consumer invoice if accessibility is significantly less than 99.95 percent of the time, 5 percent of consumer charge for every 30 minutes of downtime around 100 percent). Rather, all cloud suppliers concur in their SLAs that the burden of discovering a breach should lie only with the consumer and that consumers have a comparatively brief time to submit a claim (e.g., 1 billing month, 30 business days in the previous claim). In conclusion, the principal limitation of present SLAs is their narrow focus on just service accessibility or asked completion speed (Baset 2012). It also needs to prescribe the burden of discovering SLA offenses shared between the client and the supplier, and possibly most significant of all prerequisites, an SLA ought to be negotiable to be tailored to the user's needs and attributes. Dimension Data (2013) generated another questionnaire comparing public SLAs. Oddly, the same isn't true for cloud technologies, whose center attributes—multitenancy, on-demand provider, and place independence—create outside examinations and audits that are highly impractical and hard. However, as far as danger in SLA concerns—for audit and evaluation—the particular novelties cloud systems present continue to require regular updates and analysis.

In summary, how should a cloud-oriented evaluation and audit be done?

- On-demand self-evident: human interaction is diminished in cloud system operations; thus, an integral control point of routine audit and evaluation processes is lacking.

- Broad network accessibility: Data location freedom complicates the verification of legal compliance; the assault surface is dependent upon the absolute heterogeneity of obtaining devices and finish points.
- Resource pooling: The collection of tools set up for a given program isn't defined a priori; virtualization introduces correlation between providers sharing physical assets; the action of distinct tenants may interfere with others.
- Quick comfort: The chance for a cloud user to scale in their source pool presents a level of dynamicity which produces harder audit and evaluation.
- Measured support: The pay-per-usage paradigm average of cloud computing ensures the metering capacity is itself among the most vital resource/process to examine and audit.

Finally, a general thought about audit and evaluation emerges: Cloud computing sophistication is strictly bound with dynamicity. Conventional audit and evaluation procedures are made for (mostly) static systems or methods whose tools are configured and assigned statically. The different character of cloud technologies poses remarkable limitations to present audit and evaluation procedures and, hence, raises the danger level.

Growing concerns regarding the safety of cloud solutions would be the main reason of its interest among scholars and professionals from the definition of guidelines for the inclusion of safety requirements to SLAs. As already mentioned, the conventional practice among cloud suppliers isn't to incorporate some safety conditions, but it's very likely that the strain in this direction from standardization bodies, government agencies, and analysts will probably generate a shift in the not too distant future. The challenge would be to produce guidelines for safety monitoring; authorities who are effective in enhancing the safety level for consumers; allow, evaluate, and manage risks associated with cloud solutions, tailored to the particular needs of various users.

In Toward a Security SLA—According Cloud Tracking Service, Petcu and Craciun (2014) introduced a thorough survey of open-minded and business cloud tracking tools, which can be SLA established or security-oriented. The problem that emerges is that lots of programs exist, but not one has come to be a norm adopted by cloud suppliers and not one, likely, has reached the maturity and completeness to be integrated with conventional procedures of cloud suppliers. Besides conceptual resistances, many technical issues still need to be solved: dispersing high-tech security attributes to low-level observation parameters, effectively managing the complexity introduced by virtualization, and source elasticity are the hardest difficulties. The parameters to add in a safety SLA covered in the manual and accompanied by a discussion and illustrations are:

- Incident response
- Service comfort and load tolerance
- Data life-cycle direction
- Technical vulnerability and compliance management
- Change direction
- Data isolation
- Log direction and forensics

As an overall comment, attempts by ENISA to be proactive in suggesting practical answers have to be mentioned. Following that, however, the manual is based on several assumptions that have not yet been accepted in real SLAs; therefore, the consequence of the document appears occasionally more of a wish list for potential, advanced cloud SLAs compared to a manual for the current contracts.

In particular, two assumptions—currently mentioned in this chapter—don't reflect the current methods: that the burden of tracking and discovering SLA offenses must be shared between the cloud client and the supplier, and also cloud SLA has to be tailored to clients' threat profiles. Neither of them, as we've observed, is presently a standard in cloud SLAs. For instance, in the ENISA manual: "Parameters must be chosen in line with this use-case [...] Parameters should likewise be chosen according to an analysis of a company's main regions of risk and also the effect the IT service may have on those." Interestingly, ENISA doesn't present a set of parameters rigorously security-dependent, but a general list of prerequisites for successful management of safety (e.g., change direction and log direction are somewhat more general than safety direction, but key because of its efficacy and basic for hazard analysis).

Additionally, the incident response parameter indicates an additional attribute not mentioned before but capable of mentioning:

Incident response is flat to other parameters because episodes and coverage thresholds are described concerning the other parameters contained in the SLA. By way of instance, an incident could be increased when accessibility falls below 99.99% for 90 per cent of consumers for 1 month, even when elasticity tests neglect or if a vulnerability of a certain severity is discovered.

This may be among the greatest cases to boost the requirement that a cloud supplier be also kept responsible for SLA violations, since in this situation it isn't only an issue of quantifying the performance of several operational parameters on a per-user basis, however, but also to truly have an international measure of the way the entire cloud process is carried over the clients. A good instance of the requirement for powerful customization of a safety SLA is provided in taking risk for the support elasticity and load allowance. This parameter can also serve the requirement of occupying DoS or DDoS attacks.

On the other hand, the financial effect (losses) of DoS/DDoS is famously extremely changeable, being strictly determined by the industrial and company qualities of the sufferer. Highly static programs (e.g., running a pair of low-traffic servers without a demand variation) might not have to incorporate this requirement, though it can nevertheless be asked to guarantee resilience against DoS/DDoS strikes.

As a result, the important part of the ENISA manual, as well as the parameters that are suggested, is that there isn't any powerful security SLA without discussing the load of discovering SLA offenses between the client and the supplier, and without offering to the client the chance to tailor the SLA on his/her particular risk profile.

The CUMULUS work is very detailed and comprehensive and must be thought of as a reference manual for future safety SLA specifications. Anyhow, it cannot escape the subtleties of safety risk analysis. For example, it arouses vulnerability amounts as an important parameter to think about, not mentioned in the current SLAs, but generally assessed by associations through exposure scans, tracking tools, and penetration tests. This is a sensible observation, more general than the particular extent of an SLA.

This suggests assessing the threat posed by vulnerabilities doesn't finish with a technical evaluation, but it indicates an evaluation phase connected to the vulnerabilities' attributes, their effect (direct and indirect) on a company and surgeries, and a principle for establishing priorities.

Defining a vulnerability degree is both a technical and a managerial job, and it always suggests a choice which couldn't only be "fix all," except few little scenarios. Doing this over the years is becoming too costly, ridden with adverse effects, and also a waste of scarce resources.

Vulnerabilities have to be rated (i.e., weighted), hazard analysis must be done according to a risk acceptance standard, and a threshold has to be set up to a particular vulnerability. This is the inevitable logic supporting the quest for a dependable, robust, and sensible ranking standard for vulnerabilities. However, here the subtleties of hazard evaluation applied to vulnerabilities come into play: criteria frequently corrode because of obsolescence, their suitability has to be contested and always researched, otherwise hazard analysis too becomes unsuccessful. This is what's happening to CVSS variation 2: its validity because of a scoring system was severely criticized and for most, it's no longer regarded as a practical alternative for managing the threat posed by vulnerabilities (Allodi and Massacci 2014; Eiram and Martin n.d.; Freund and Jones 2014; Rothke 2015).

This chapter contributed to danger in cloud systems, a subject that's the topic of several studies, investigations, and polls since the ancient days of cloud systems. However, as with risk and data security (which mostly overlaps with hazard in cloud systems), investigations, taxonomies, and the same language are still far away from maturity. Instead, language is frequently context dependent or overly generic, and we're still fighting with a transparent identification of which dangers are odd to cloud technologies and thus need new investigations, strategies, and alternatives, and that are dangers of cloud building blocks like an open network, remote accesses, cryptographic procedures, and Internet technologies.

Multitenancy and on-demand adaptive provision of tools are the other features of cloud systems, the most examined due to their specificity and influence on dangers. When calculating hazard management, along with references to risk management criteria from global organizations, the attention of a massive body of investigations and researches is your contractual relationship that governs cloud solutions and enables the transfer of dangers from a cloud client to a cloud supplier. The definition of an SLA between the parties would be the approved way to specify the states of the arrangement, but for cloud technologies, there's a continuous debate about present SLAs, which can be deemed mainly inadequate particularly for shielding clients from cloud dangers.

REFERENCES

Allodi, L., and F. Massacci. 2014. "Comparing Vulnerability Severity and Exploits Using Case–Control Studies." *ACM Transactions on Information and System Security* 17, no. 1, p. 1.

Baset, S.A. 2012. "Cloud SLAs: Present and Future." *ACM SIGOPS Operating Systems Review* 46, no. 2, pp. 57–66.

Bennani, N., E. Damiani, and S. Cimato. 2010. Toward Cloud–based Key Management for Outsourced Databases. *Proceedings of the 34th Annual IEEE Computer Software and Applications Conference Workshop*, July 19–23, Seoul, South Korea.

Brender, N., and I. Markov. 2013. "Risk Perception and Risk Management in Cloud Computing: Results From a Case Study of Swiss Companies." *International Journal of Information Management* 33, no. 5, pp. 726–33.

Carlson, F.R. 2014. "Security Analysis of Cloud Computing." arXiv Preprint, arXiv:1404.6849.

Carroll, M., A. Van Der Merwe, and P. Kotze. 2011. Secure Cloud Computing: Benefits, Risks and Controls. *Proceedings of the 2011 Information Security for South Africa (ISSA)*. August 15–17, IEEE, Johannesburg, South Africa.

Claycomb, W.R., and A. Nicoll. 2012. Insider Threats to Cloud Computing: Directions for New Research Challenges. *Proceedings of the IEEE 36th Annual Computer Software and Applications Conference (COMPSAC)*, July 16–20, Izmir, Turkey.

Cramer, R., I. Damgård, and J.B. Nielsen. 2001. *Multiparty Computation from Threshold Homomorphic Encryption*. Berlin, Germany: Springer.

Damiani, E., S. Cimato, and G. Gianini. 2015. "A Risk Model for Cloud Processes." *ISC International Journal of Information Security* 6, no. 2, pp. 99–123.

Dimension Data. 2013. "Comparing Public Cloud Service Level Agreements. White Paper." https://www.slideshare.net/DidataCloud/comparing-public-cloud-service-level-agreements-white-paper (accessed July 24, 2015).

Eiram, C., and B. Martin. n.d. The CVSSv2 Shortcomings, Faults, and Failures Formulation—An Open Letter to FIRST. https://www.riskbasedsecurity.com/reports/CVSS-ShortcomingsFaultsandFailures.pdf, (accessed July 25, 2015).

Freund, J., and J. Jones. 2014. *Measuring and Managing Information Risk: A FAIR Approach*. Oxford, England: Butterworth-Heinemann.

Gentry, C. 2009. Fully Homomorphic Encryption Using Ideal Lattices. *Proceedings of the Forty-first Annual ACM Symposium on Theory of Computing*, May 31 to June 2, Bethesda, MD.

ISO/FDIS. 2009. *ISO/FDIS 31000:2009 Risk Management—Principles and Guidelines on Implementation*. Geneva, Switzerland: ISO/FDIS.

ISO/IEC. 2009. *ISO/IEC 27000:2009 Information Technology—Security Techniques—Information Security Management Systems—Overview and Vocabulary*. Geneva, Switzerland: ISO/IEC.

Janeczko, J. 2011. "Risk Analysis Framework for a Cloud Specific Environment. White Paper," *Atos*. https://atos.net/content/dam/global/we-do/atos-cloud-risk-analysis-white-paper.pdf, (accessed July 14, 2015).

Keller, R., and C. König. 2014. A Reference Model to Support Risk Identification in Cloud Networks. *Proceedings of the 35th International Conference on Information Systems (ICIS)*, December 14–17, Auckland, New Zealand.

Knight, F. H. 1921. *Risk, Uncertainty and Profit*. New York, NY: Hart, Schaffner and Marx.

Knight, F.H. 2012. *Risk, Uncertainty and Profit*. New York, NY: Courier Corporation.

López-Alt, A., E. Tromer, and V. Vaikuntanathan. 2012. On–the–fly Multiparty Computation on the Cloud via Multikey Fully Homomorphic Encryption. *Proceedings of the 44th Annual ACM Symposium on Theory of Computing*, May 20–21, New York, NY.

Mell, P., and T. Grance. 2011. "The NIST Definition of Cloud Computing," NIST Special Publication 800-145, NIST.

Moore, A.P., D.M. Capelli, T.C. Caron, E. Shaw, D. Spooner, and R.F. Trzeciak. 2011. "A Preliminary Model of Insider Theft of Intellectual Property." *Journal of Wireless Mobile Networks, Ubiquitous Computing, and Dependable Applications* 2, no. 1, pp. 28–49.

NIST. 2011. "Managing Information Security Risk: Organization, Mission, and Information System View," Special Publication 800-39, Joint Task Force Transformation Initiative.

Petcu, D., and C. Craciun. 2014. Towards a Security SLA–based Cloud Monitoring Service. *Proceedings of the 4th International Conference on Cloud Computing and Services Science (CLOSER)*, April 3–5, Barcelona, Spain.

Rong, C., S.T. Nguyen, and M. Gilje Jaatun. 2013. "Beyond Lightning: A Survey on Security Challenges in Cloud Computing." *Computers & Electrical Engineering* 39, no. 1, pp. 47–54.

Rothke, B. 2015. "How to Get CVSS Right." CSO Online. http://www.csoonline.com/article/2910312/application-security/how-to-get-cvssright.html (accessed July 25, 2015).

Ryan, M.D. 2013. "Cloud Computing Security: The Scientific Challenge, and a Survey of Solutions." *Journal of Systems and Software* 86, no. 9, pp. 2263–68.

Saripalli, P., and B. Walters. 2010. QUIRC: A Quantitative Impact and Risk Assessment Framework for Cloud Security. *Proceedings of the IEEE 3rd International Conference on Cloud Computing (CLOUD)*, July 5–10, Miami, FL.

Stone, G., and P. Noel. n.d. "Cloud Risk Decision Framework." *Microsoft.* http://download.microsoft.com/documents/australia/enterprise/SMIC1545_PDF_v7_pdf.pdf, (accessed July 23, 2015).

Theoharidou, M., N. Papanikolaou, S. Pearson, and D. Gritzalis. 2013. Privacy Risk, Security, Accountability in the Cloud. *Proceedings of the IEEE 5th International Conference on Cloud Computing Technology and Science (CloudCom)*, December 2–5, Bristol, England.

Von Neumann, J., and O. Morgenstern. 2007. *Theory of Games and Economic Behavior*. Princeton, NJ: Princeton University Press.

Yanpei, C., V. Paxson, and R.H. Katz. 2010. What's New about Cloud Computing Security. Report No. UCB/EECS-2010-5, University of California, Berkeley, CA.

CHAPTER 12

INFRASTRUCTURE-AS-A-SERVICE (IAAS)

To be able to use the fundamentals of data security to any cloud structure, it's essential to understand the cloud architecture. Within this chapter, we'll examine some of the significant constituents of cloud infrastructure and also a few notions to help us consider the safety of the structure. Knowing how security controls and practices operate in a cloud surrounding will permit us to employ the ideal sorts of safety to satisfy our risk tolerance for virtually any circumstance.

12.1. CONSIDERATIONS

As we believe security from an individual view of cloud infrastructure, it will be valuable to think about the larger picture of how the performance of this cloud infrastructure as a whole can affect us as a consumer of the cloud (Gurkok 2013). In managing cloud surroundings in support of numerous customers, the cloud operator should satisfy the security demands of most users of the surroundings. These various users will typically have different safety requirements, too. The idea of the largest common denominator dictating the cloud environment has to be the superset of requirements required of all customers, knowing there is not any user that requires each of these requirements. One way to decrease the complexity overhead in this sort of circumstance would be to isolate unique groups of renters or software into different communities, according to their various security requirements. The trick to the method is to find users with similar safety conditions and set them together. A new overarching concept that's important to remember is the notion of shared impacts like the ones associated with strikes on or failures of their shared infrastructure.

In these sections, we'll have a peek at what sorts of tools are distributed and managed using a cloud infrastructure (National Institute of Standards and Technology 2011). A cloud infrastructure typically handles many nodes running a much more significant number of cases. Each case may be committed to one workload or operate multiple workloads if proper. Possibly the most usual sort of virtualization is that of a hypervisor. The hypervisor's function is to handle the access to physical tools, dividing the CPU and RAM and storage into one of the virtualized machines—the calculate cases—which are operating on the physical calculate node handled by this hypervisor. A container isolates software by maintaining their consumer spaces different while letting them share one kernel space. It's more complicated but more lightweight than the usual hardware hypervisor. A bare-metal compute element manages workloads with no virtualization. Each workload is conducted on another piece of hardware.

A hypervisor may fail to keep this rigorous isolation if, by way of instance, it's vulnerable to some breakout strike, in which malicious code running in a single virtual machine may break from their virtualized environment and require a charge of the hypervisor itself and consequently control all of the virtual machines handled by this hypervisor. Less dramatic but equally impactful is a vulnerable hypervisor that enables a virtual machine to get the contents of a memory used by a different virtual machine on precisely the same host to calculate node. Both these kinds of vulnerabilities along with some other vulnerabilities have been discovered previously, although none of these applies to current versions of almost any popular hypervisor or containers.

It is also important to think about resource exhaustion. A malicious user may cripple the cloud infrastructure, or impact performance for different users of the infrastructure, by swallowing the CPU and RAM resources supplied by computing nodes. This type of vulnerability is mostly not appropriate to bare-metal compute nodes since CPU and RAM resources aren't shared among multiple workloads. Regardless, it's essential to get ready for this potential, whether due to malicious intent or merely a workload or program that matches out of control. One crucial final safety consideration is that of the operational trust version of a cloud infrastructure. Particularly with the hypervisor strategy, the supervisor of a cloud computing infrastructure has the power to invisibly view, copy, and change the information contained in, and activities performed utilizing a workload or program running in that cloud atmosphere. Because of this, it's essential to perform a comprehensive evaluation of any third parties involved in handling the cloud infrastructure, even more than in the circumstance of a traditional colocation structure.

12.2. NETWORK

The system element of a cloud infrastructure permits connectivity of one of the computers, storage, and other components of the infrastructure, in addition to the broader environment beyond that infrastructure. At a minimum, the system part joins the network centers of the calculate element to the border of this cloud environment and oversees the type of accessibility the calculate cases have between each other and also into the broader environment.

Beyond that minimum necessary capacity, there are numerous methods to handle the system topology at a cloud infrastructure: digital shifting, the direction of physical network gear, and software-defined media.

12.3. SECURITY IMPLICATIONS

Like calculate elements, the maximum security-critical obligation of the network part is isolation. For instance, the network part has to avoid malicious workloads from getting unauthorized VLANs and subnets, which might be available by approved workloads sharing the same physical hardware.

At a minimum, the storage unit stores cloud control data, such as virtual server and digital system definitions, and provides working distance to software and workloads running in the cloud atmosphere. Past the minimal requirement to conduct a workload in cloud surroundings, the storage element as implemented by the majority of contemporary cloud infrastructure technologies may offer various additional capacities for innovative operational capabilities or to boost management advantage.

A contemporary storage element can implement version or backup control by working together with the hypervisors to make a snapshot at fixed intervals and keep them based on the configured backup scheme. Another way the storage element can collaborate with all the hypervisors or containers would be to allow for workload migration among server compute nodes. Notably, for a distributed workload in large scales, technical storage may radically simplify the workload execution. These unique storage mechanisms are generally implemented as item stores. There's a fine line between complex storage element performance and performance more correctly credited to the database part. For instance, we'll discuss key-value shops in Section 12.4, but these can be implemented by precisely the same element that provides more conventional storage mechanisms.

12.4. STORAGE

Much like other elements of a cloud structure, possibly the most crucial security-related consideration requires complete isolation between computer cases, workloads, and software. In the event of storage, the calculate element has a significant part in enforcing that solitude; nonetheless, the storage element must also guarantee that computer cases can access only licensed storage areas, such as by minding robust network file system permissions and iSCSI authentication. Malicious code on a single calculate case shouldn't be able to get another workload information by manipulating the storage infrastructure. These issues spread to additional, more complicated facets of the storage part's performance too.

Mismanaged permissions along with other standard information hygiene jobs are a primary source of danger in almost any surrounding—all the more so at a cloud infrastructure given the complicated, multitenant character of those infrastructures. By providing this vital service for a suitable level of abstraction, the database element enables the software and workloads running in cloud surroundings to utilize support for its database requirements, making them more accessible and more straightforward to implement.

The database element implements database performance that isn't just pure for software to leverage, but that will climb as the workload increases along with the cloud; the program raises the requirements it puts on the database layer. At the very least, the database part offers shared access to a centrally controlled database program, whether SQL or even NoSQL. Most robust database elements permit users to instantiate database providers as demanded by their workloads, while allowing the cloud infrastructure owner to control specific areas of the database, including backup programs, or performance and capacity parameters. (Yeluri and Castro-Leon 2014)

The driving requirement behind every cloud based database is the fact that cloud-oriented applications frequently need an ability to scale up and down based on the way the workload needs of this program change over time.

A standard SQL database isn't designed from the ground up to scale in reaction to real-time workload variations. We won't spend much time covering them. Instead, we'll cover alternative databasing techniques like key-value shops and chart databases, which tend to be more straightforward to execute in a scalable way, and about which much of this evolution of cloud database elements have been oriented.

Document-oriented databases are a popular technology in cloud surroundings. These databases are occasionally known as data structure shops since they deal in data which are structured much because it would be from the sense of a standard programming language.

Key-value databases are also a highly popular choice in cloud surroundings. The values within a key-value database could be complicated ones, like dictionaries or hashes. Graph databases store information as a set of nodes linked by associations, explicitly preserving the interconnections among different data points. Social networks are just one. As the technology evolves, the database part of cloud computing architectures will create dispersed databasing scale simpler and stronger than earlier ones.

12.5. DATABASES

Contrary to the other elements of a cloud structure, databases have had the requirement to isolate users from each other and also to configure specific access permissions on an intricate data collection to an intricate user base. However, databases are utilized to store data, which is frequently one of the most significant assets of a contemporary enterprise. Because of this, it's essential to take into account the worth of the info stored in a cloud infrastructure.

Irrespective of the technologies involved, we're expecting third parties to have the most crucial asset within our business. Mitigating technology like encryption is beyond the range of this segment, but frequently forms an essential component of a secure database element within a cloud infrastructure.

12.6. CONTROL

The direction element of a cloud infrastructure provides the means by which administrators and users may configure and operate each of the handled facets of the infrastructure. To be able to attain this, it has to first have the ability to communicate with every element, implementing operation that incorporates profoundly with compute, storage, network, and even database elements. These functions have to be subjected to the users in addition to the administrators of this cloud infrastructure.

A user-facing front-end program, generally in the kind of an Internet program, gives the graphical user an interface for manual setup and functionality. However, this type of standard interface doesn't scale up to big cloud infrastructures; it's imperative the management element exposes its functionality through some programmatic interface which simplifies the automation of regular activities for cloud infrastructure management and functionality.

All contemporary management element implementations support some application programming interface (API) for only such automation. APIs are also arguably the most complicated portion of a cloud infrastructure to correctly protected. This is both due to the complexity of the operations done by the management element and because of the numerous interface factors the direction element has to support. The management element can perform all of the configuration tasks required to prepare and run the cloud infrastructure. To do so, it has to handle multiple compute nodes, storage back-ends, community link, and database suppliers.

The management element has to authenticate unique users, comprehend each user's part in the functioning of the cloud environment, and monitor many complex authorization dependencies to restrict the tasks a user can perform appropriately. Moreover, the management element has to expose its complicated capability set employing a user-oriented graphical user interface along with also a machine-oriented API. Every one of those exposure approaches brings its safety concerns, from input to business rule enforcement. It's crucial to comprehend the solid additional strike surface and functioning sophistication a strong management element attracts.

Cloud infrastructures can be exceedingly complicated, yet it's essential to know them intimately to secure clouds correctly. It's not possible to cover the subject thoroughly in one chapter, but this ought to be sufficient to set the info in the remainder of this publication into the appropriate context.

REFERENCES

Gurkok, C. 2013. "Securing Cloud Computing Systems." In *Computer and Information Security Handbook*, ed. J.R. Vacca. 2nd ed. Boston, MA: Elsevier, pp. 97–123.

National Institute of Standards and Technology. 2011. "The NIST Definition of Cloud Computing," Special Publication 800-145.

Yeluri, R., and E. Castro-Leon. 2014. *Building the Infrastructure for Cloud Security*. New York, NY: Apress Media, pp. 160–63.

CHAPTER 13

CRYPTOGRAPHIC KEY MANAGEMENT FOR DATA PROTECTION

Public and private sector organizations, as well as individuals, have been transferring considerable quantities of data to the cloud in the last 10 years. This is true even though basically, cloud computing has uncertainties that cause unique security challenges compared with traditional information technology environments such as data centers—uncertainties that arise because of inherently remote operations, chances of cotenancy and shared/distributed direction, and administrative control. Cryptography is a vital technology to secure cloud operations. The use of cryptography suggests the use of cryptographic keys. While cryptographic keys help to guard the safety of information, the keys themselves also need to be protected to ensure they are not released to or altered by unauthorized entities and are stored by authorized entities to allow access to the information. Cryptographic keys need to be managed throughout their life cycle to safeguard their confidentiality, integrity, and availability—basically, they are as precious as the collective value of each of the data they protect. Thus, sound techniques for managing the life cycle of those keys are crucial to the security of the general cryptographic infrastructure. Within this chapter, we'll describe the foundational theories in cryptographic key management, the layout choices for key management methods, the challenges of key direction in cloud systems, and strategies for implementing successful key management inside the cloud.

There are many uncertainties inside a clouded atmosphere. It's often unknown in which clouded atmosphere the user's process is running at any time or where the user's information is stored. It's possible that the user's process is sharing a chip with a different user's procedure or that data from two consumers are coresident on the same virtual storage device. It is often unclear who has administrative access to this cloud infrastructure or the information and audit records for a particular user. Additionally, cloud environments often engender a more diverse group of threat agents and risk events because of the inherently shared nature of the environments and the presence of a larger group of actors who have access to the shared atmosphere. Within this domain of uncertainty and danger, cryptography is an especially useful technical instrument to safeguard data and transactions within a cloud environment. Asymmetric (public/private) and secret key cryptography are equally useful within a cloud surrounding (Barker, Smid, Branstad, and Chokhan 2012 and Chandramouli, Iorga, and Chokhani 2013). While public and secret keys are helpful for confidentiality protection, private and secret keys are helpful for entity authentication and integrity protection of data.

Cryptographic techniques can support many security functions inside a cloud surrounding, including:

- Remote authentication of an individual into a cloud service using single or multifactor techniques
- Assessing the confidentiality and integrity of communication and messaging protocols between cloud celebrities (e.g., SSL/TLS protected session between a browser and a distant cloud server)
- Partitioning user information in cotenant cloud surroundings (e.g., every user's data are encrypted with a user-specific secret in a frequent cloud storage apparatus)
- Protecting the confidentiality of consumer information out of privileged users (e.g., encrypted user information are protected from program administrators)

This chapter focuses on theories and methods for the effective management of cryptographic keys used to protect data in the cloud.

Cryptographic keys possess a lifespan cycle that contains some or all of the following states as illustrated in Figure 13.1.

These theories include:

- Crucial production—Creating or establishing a new cryptographic key
- Key distribution—Making a key accessible to other approved entities that need it through different methods of crucial sharing

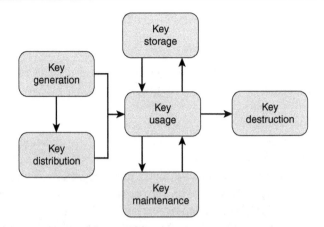

Figure 13.1. Cryptographic keys possess a lifespan cycle that contains some or all of the following states

- Key utilization—Applying a secret key for proper security operations such as encryption, decryption, digital signature, and message authentication
- Key storage—Saving a secret key to a storage medium for present or future usage
- Essential maintenance—Support operations such as key archival, recovery, renewal, and revocation throughout the life cycle of the critical data
- Key destruction—Terminating the ability to apply a key for future cryptographic operations

A key may be formatted for later recovery; retrieval comprises methods for getting another copy of a key when the primary copy of the key is corrupted or lost. Renewal enables a key to be used beyond the first period of activation. Revocation uses a key (for many different reasons) during the period of activation. For every one of these crucial life cycle stages, there is an assortment of available alternatives and decisions that impact the safety of the key in addition to the data or transactions the key was made to protect. Key management is a phrase that encompasses the total of parameters and actions related to sustaining the key through each of the life cycle phases including generation, storage, distribution, usage, recovery, and destruction. The specific set of essential management parameters and activities determine the strength and assurance of their security functions attained within a cryptographic infrastructure.

13.1. KEY MANAGEMENT SYSTEM DESIGN CHOICES

In designing a successful key management platform for data encryption keys, there are many options that are possible for all the stages of the key life cycle as explained below:

- Key generation—Crucial type (symmetric/asymmetric), algorithms, key strength, crypto period, key parameters, hardware or software crypto module, the source of entropy, etc.
- Key storage—Where saved, proximity to encrypted information, how shielded, access management, auditability, etc.
- Crucial distribution—How exchanged, distributed, and established, how protected in transit, how things are authenticated, etc.
- Key use—Granularity and volume of data to be protected, access to the key, the crypto module used for operations, how secure during and after use, etc.
- Essential upkeep—What keys will need to be recovered, who wants to recover keys, how quickly, how long keys need to be assessed, and how key retrieval is audited, whether multiparty approvals are needed, etc.
- Fundamental destruction—Once destroyed, how ruined, audit ability, etc.

These design choices impact the functionality, performance, and safety of the total system. It's best practice to develop a Knowledge Management Plan (KMP) that defines the objectives of the essential management infrastructure in addition to a critical Knowledge Management Practices Statement (KMPS) that describes the parameters and processes selected to meet the goals within the KMP. The KMP/KMPS need to deal with crucial fundamental management life cycle states and each one of the critical management design decisions made.

The design choices for an essential management infrastructure that supports encoded information within a cloud system should be made in the circumstance of the desired operational, economic, performance, compliance, and security objectives for this cloud system.

View the descriptions below:

- Functional objectives—What are the core operational aims of the platform to which cryptographic protection is going to be implemented? Is the system designed to create the very same data available to multiple users or a single user? Is the system supporting a business or a public base? How valuable or significant is the service or data the system is supporting?

- Economic goals—What are the cost limitations that are pertinent to the system? What is the most effective utilization of the budget for implementing the system?
- Performance goals—What are the goal performance parameters for the system? Is the system designed for high speed or higher volume trades? Is the system expected to be used by a high number of simultaneous users?
- Compliance objectives—What policies and mandates use to the machine based on its industry vertical, possession, and performance? How do these requirements impact the technical and the operational and management aspects of the system?
- Security goals—what's the criticality of this system? Which are the related threat events and agents? What are the present vulnerabilities? What's the amount of acceptable risk? What are the techniques to mitigate risk to deliver it inside the acceptable degree?

Figure 13.2 shows a notional decision flowchart for a cloud platform. Functional and economic objectives might drive the selection of appropriate cloud versions and support types such as:

- Cloud shipping model—Personal cloud, community cloud, public cloud, or even a hybrid of those other versions
- Cloud service kind—Processing services or storage solutions

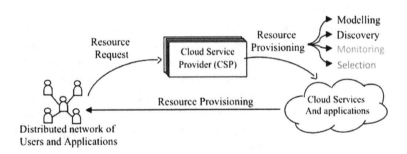

Figure 13.2. Notional decision flowchart for a cloud platform

Once a cloud model has been selected, compliance and performance goals may induce the definition of the structure of the overall cloud system. Simultaneously with cloud design decisions, the security architecture of the cloud system needs to be defined and might be driven by compliance and security objectives. Technical architectural decisions include areas of authentication, access control, usage of cryptography, auditing mechanisms, use of the secure link, and messaging protocols and methods for application security. When cryptography is used within the machine, it is essential to develop the critical proper management policies and practices to the system.

13.2.   CLOUD KEY MANAGEMENT CHALLENGES

However, there are specific challenges in developing a key management system for encoded data inside a cloud environment. Some of the most significant challenges include:

- Authentication of remote users—As mentioned previously, each user of a cloud-based system is a "distant" user who links to the cloud network over a shared medium. To allow remote users to access encrypted data stored on the cloud system, the consumer has to be authenticated at an assurance level commensurate with the strength of the encryption employed.
- Hardware versus software cryptography—Cloud technologies are designed for elasticity, rapid deployment, and possible use by multiple cloud customers. These characteristics make it very difficult for cloud support providers to provide cryptographic services that use hardware cryptographic modules; the standard for cloud systems would be to use software instead. This can pose a problem for some cloud consumers who are required by law to use hardware cryptography.
- Multiple layers of privileged customers—Unlike systems hosted within an organization-owned data center, cloud systems are based on layers of platform and infrastructure services that are potentially offered by disparate cloud service providers. Each layer of cloud services comprises privileged administrators and users along with the privileged administrators and users which are a part of the cloud consumer organization. These multiple collections of privileged users pose an unusually high degree of insider threat for cloud systems.
- Multitenancy—Most cloud systems are created for multitenancy, encouraging many cloud consumers through a shared infrastructure, platform, or program services. The information and procedures of those multiple tenants are separated through software mechanisms within the application layer (for SaaS), platform layer (such as PaaS), and hypervisor layer (for IaaS).

- Availability of information and keys—Encryption is typically reserved for sensitive and critical data. When such information resides within a cloud system, there may be challenges in ensuring that the encrypted data and the related keys are always available.

Cloud key management systems need to be designed with due consideration to these extraordinary challenges present within cloud systems.

13.3. CLOUD KEY MANAGEMENT STRATEGIES

On account of the safety challenges inherent in cloud systems, it might be required to use cryptographic techniques more often than in private data centers to safeguard sensitive or critical data saved in the cloud. In this section, we investigate some approaches for cloud key management. Therefore, it is highly advisable to perform an analysis to identify the data that are worthy of being cryptographically protected, then prioritize the need for cryptography of their information with the highest worth or criticality. The goal is to minimize the information collection that has to be protected through cryptographic keys.

Separate Ciphertext from Keys on accounts shows how the cloud user has less control over where their keys or saved data, and how the cloud user has the ability to obtain access to them. It is advisable to look for a cloud security system so the ciphertext (encrypted data) from the keys may be used to decrypt the ciphertext. This approach may be potential in an IaaS cloud service but may be hard or not possible within a PaaS or SaaS cloud support.

To the extent possible (while retaining the operational, economic, and performance goals of the cloud system in standpoint), the level of separation of the ciphertext from the related keys should be increased inside a cloud platform. Some of the probable choices for separation of ciphertext and related keys are as follows.

13.3.1. ESTABLISH TRUST IN CRYPTO MODULE

The data and keys are available in the crypto module when a cryptographic operation is being done. Therefore, the cloud user needs to establish a degree of trust; the crypto module being used cannot be readily endangered to produce sensitive or keys data out there for ingestion by rogue parties. This may imply using hardware crypto modules in the cloud (when possible) or using trusted crypto modules run by the cloud customer business or trusted third parties offering such services.

13.3.2. USE KEY SPLITTING TECHNIQUES

When available or possible, cryptographic key dividing techniques may be utilized with cloud essential management systems to make sure that the cloud provider doesn't have easy access to the full keys used to protect sensitive data. In such implementations, a part of this key may be saved within the cloud system along with another part saved in a trustworthy appliance or third-party support. Only the cloud user can join the parts of the essential together to perform cryptographic operations on sensitive information.

Protecting sensitive and high-value data within a cloud system necessitates the use of cryptographic techniques and cryptographic keys. The direction of those keys is particularly challenging in cloud environments due to the extended exposure to several insider and outsider threat agents. Some commonsense design choices and strategies can help to implement secure and effective key management methods to protect information stored in the cloud.

REFERENCES

Barker, E., M. Smid, D. Branstad, and S. Chokhan. 2012. "A Framework for Designing Cryptographic Key Management Systems," NIST Special Publication 800-130.

Chandramouli, R., M. Iorga, and S. Chokhani. 2013. "NISTIR 7956 Cryptographic Key Management Issues & Challenges in Cloud Services. NIST.".

CHAPTER 14

MANAGING LEGAL COMPLIANCE RISK AND PERSONAL DATA PROTECTION

Together with the widespread use of technologies and the evermore important role it plays in business, the adoption of cloud computing technology is growing at an unprecedented speed. According to Eurostat, in 2014, 24 percent of large enterprises made use of public cloud computing services (Eurostat 2014), and Gartner predicts the strongly marked public cloud growth to continue, with an expected 18 percent increase to "almost $250 billion by 2017, including cloud advertising" (Anderson et al. 2013).

The vast majority of big businesses have already moved into the cloud as a consequence of its high capacity to enhance productivity, streamline information processing, and possibly above all decrease costs and increase margins. The US Federal Government has also recognized the power of cloud computing, exemplified in the federal cloud computing strategy that was designed as an outline for the adoption of cloud services by the government itself (Kundra 2011, p. 2).

The Asia Cloud Computing Association, an industry association that represents cloud ecosystem stakeholders in Asia, recently released a report titled "Asia's financial services. Ready for the Cloud—A Report on FSI Regulations Impacting Cloud in Asia-Pacific Markets," which covers the regulatory landscape for the cloud in Asia-Pacific and identifies regulatory obstacles in the adoption of cloud services in the financial services industry.

Based on their findings, the authors suggest five main recommendations for lawmakers:

1. There should be no separate regulations for the use of cloud providers.
2. Regulations should set a transparent process which needs to be followed to the adoption of cloud solutions (as if it were some other

form of outsourcing) and no endorsement should be required for the utilization of cloud services.

3. The transfer of data into other authorities must be permitted, subject to proper safeguards (e.g., safety, business continuity, access, and audit).
4. Regulations should only identify the critical issues that should be addressed in outsourcing contracts which include cloud solutions. They shouldn't be prescriptive of the terms of an outsourcing contract which provides cloud services.
5. The use of independent third-party audits should be an acceptable alternative to audits carried out by financial services institutions (FSIs) and the regulators (Asia Cloud Computing Association 2015).

While the benefits of cloud computing technologies undoubtedly outweigh the risks, it is of utmost importance that the legal and regulatory aspects are fully understood and analyzed. In 2012, the European Commission adopted its "Unleashing the Potential of Cloud Computing in Europe" cloud computing strategy (European Commission 2012), which was last updated on February 27, 2015. The strategy itself is the final product of policy, technology and regulatory landscape analysis, and stakeholder consultation. The strategy aims to improve European GDP by 1 percent by 2020 as well as to create 2.5 million jobs in the EU by way of cloud adoption across a wide range of sectors. The strategy focuses on three main actions, namely (i) cutting through the jungle of standards, (ii) safe and fair contract terms and conditions, and (iii) the establishment of a European Cloud Partnership to drive innovation and growth from the public sector (European Commission 2012). We will now take a glance at each of these three main actions. First of all, we should look at the so-called jungle of standards.

The maze of standards present in the regulatory sphere represents one of the most significant challenges to the development of the cloud (OECD 2014, p. 5). In fact, the plethora of standards we can observe generate uncertainty concerning adequate levels of personal data protection, interoperability, and portability, and for this reason the European Cloud Strategy aims to establish publicly available clouds that are both open and secure in full compliance with European regulatory standards (European Commission 2012, pp. 5–6). In the digital world, issues are often intertwined. Take, for example, the Digital Agenda's e-commerce Directive, which demonstrates that a primary hindrance in the adoption of the cloud is "the lack of appropriate standards in some areas, the lack of widespread adoption of existing standards and the potential for vendor lock-in due to the use of non-interoperable solutions" (European Commission 2012, p. 7). Organization of the jungle of standards would allow for adequate interoperability, data portability, and reversibility, critical considerations in the adoption of cloud computing services (Digital Agenda for Europe 2015). This will be achieved through the European Data Protection Regulation, a framework law that will foster an environment that allows for the safe adoption of standards and codes of conduct that users need to successfully verify security standards and the security of data transfers (European Commission 2012, p. 8). Cutting through the jungle of rules would mean allowing cloud users to experience interoperability, data portability, and, importantly, reversibility (Digital Agenda for Europe 2015).

Trust plays an essential role in cloud adoption, and in fact, the digital single market approach itself highlights the energy of this identification "of a proper set of criteria that can be certified in order to allow public and private procurers to be confident that they have met their compliance duties" (European Commission 2012, p. 9). These standards and certifications, in turn, can be referenced as the terms and conditions supplied by cloud support suppliers for contractual fairness and transparency. As the Commission has pointed out, nevertheless, in its "Unleashing the Potential of Cloud Computing in Europe communication," there's a need for specific frameworks that deal with both criteria and certifications as well as contract stipulations.

According to the commission, the objective of this cloud computing strategy would be the development of model contracts which would regulate:

1. Data preservation following the conclusion of the contract
2. Data disclosure and integrity
3. Data location and transfer
4. Ownership of the information
5. Direct and indirect liability change of service by cloud suppliers and subcontracting

14.1. DIGITAL AGENDA FOR EUROPE 2015

The European Cloud Partnership was established under the European Cloud Strategy to act as a place where industry and the public sector "work on common procurement requirements for cloud computing in an open and fully transparent way" (Digital Agenda for Europe 2014). Its steering board provides advice to the commission to facilitate the positive effects of the cloud in the economy, stressing the importance of the public sector as a defining aspect of the cloud market (Digital Agenda for Europe 2014a).

Moreover, the OECD stresses in "Cloud Computing: The Concept, Impacts and the Role of Government Policy" that standard contracts are often on take-it-or-leave-it terms, thereby not allowing the cloud customer to adequately negotiate the contract terms that the client may not fully understand, resulting in considerable uncertainty even for the providers. Service-level agreements (SLAs) need to address better aspects such as the outage, which could be promoted in policy through the concretization of industry codes of conduct (OECD 2014, p. 5).

Regarding privacy, the OECD observes that a genuinely global interoperable approach on the part of governments is the key to maximizing the potential for cloud deployment, suggesting that policymakers define "whose laws apply to the data stored in the cloud, including who can access this data" (OECD 2014, p. 6). Bradshaw, Millard, and Walden (2010, p. 44) emphasize the importance of careful examination of cloud contract terms and conditions specified for disclosure, data storage location, which is not always considered in contracts outside of the EU, and the identity of underlying service providers.

The terms and conditions of many cloud computing contracts represent legal challenges for the adoption of cloud services. This is underlined by Bradshaw, Millard, and Walden whose research on the terms and conditions offered by cloud computing providers demonstrates that standard cloud contracts, in fact, provide a shallow level of certainty in comparison to outsourcing contracts (2010, p. 3). This chapter is inspired by the author's participation in two projects, CloudWATCH D3.5 Legal Guide to the Cloud: How to Protect Personal Data in Cloud Service Contracts[1] and Cloud Security Alliance's Privacy Level Agreement [V2] A Compliance Tool for Providing Cloud Services in the European Union,[2] each of which explores fundamental aspects of cloud computing contracts relevant to the study undertaken herein. Drawing heavily on this experience, the author aims to further an understanding of the legal compliance risk in the cloud, how it can be managed, as well as to touch on aspects that should be considered when negotiating personal data protection risks with vendors of

---

[1]CloudWATCH is a European cloud observatory that supports cloud policies, standard profiles, and services. The European Commission's Unit funds it on Software and Services, Cloud Computing within DG Connect under the 7th Framework Program. More information can be found at http://www.cloudwatchhub.eu/ and at http://www.cloudwatchhub.eu/sites/default/files/Guidelines%20on%20how%20to%20protect%20personal%20 data%20in%20 cloud%20service%20contracts_0_0.pdf

[2]The Cloud Security Alliance is a premier organization that defines and raises awareness of best practices to have a cloud computing environment. The first version of the privacy level agreement (PLA) was published in 2013 as a self-regulatory harmonization tool offering a structured mode of communication at the level of personal data protection put forth by a cloud provider to customers and potential customers.

cloud services. While the promotion of a global understanding of the matter is the objective of this chapter, due to his position as a European lawyer, the author will primarily perform the analysis from an EU compliance perspective.

14.2. ADDRESSING LEGAL COMPLIANCE

The prosperity of cloud computing technologies and services develops in unison with all the various manners of delivering IT services that are made possible thanks to its significant diffusion of cellular apparatus as previously mentioned. Companies, in fact, in contemplating hybrid solutions can buy services according to their needs, fitting obvious and personal private cloud solutions (Gartner 2013).

Legal versions have developed together with the proliferation of these technologies, albeit at a much slower pace. Increased attention, however, is being paid to cloud computing contracts, which frequently continue to be phrased in standard forms by cloud providers. It's important for customers of cloud solutions to pay proper attention to the next contractual aspects:

- Exclusion or limitation of liability and remedies, especially concerning data integrity and disaster recovery
- Service levels, also including availability
- Security and privacy, in particular, regulatory issues under the European Union Data Protection Directive[3]
- Lock-in and exit, including the duration, termination rights, and return of data when exiting the contract
- The ability of the provider to unilaterally modify service features[4]

14.2.1. PRECONTRACTUAL PHASE

This section (CloudWATCH 2014) is intended as a guide for potential customers in their compliance evaluation of cloud services. It isolates the principal issues linked to the three stages of the cloud connection which include the precontractual phase, the contractual phase, and the postcontractual phase. All the aspects are discussed in more detail below and integrated with useful checklists which could be utilized to help the customer make an educated choice.

---

[3]EUR-Lex (1995) (after this Directive 95/46/EC).
[4]These issues have been identified by Hon, Millard, and Walden (2012).

14.2.2.   STEP 1: PRECONTRACTUAL PHASE

The prerequisite contractual period or the phase before the contract is signed a significant time in advance to any contractual arrangement. It is essential that the client is supplied with adequate and transparent information concerning all elements of the cloud contract to best avoid litigation later on (Helberger and Verite 2014).

14.2.3.   RISKS AND OPPORTUNITIES FOR YOUR CLOUD SERVICE CLIENT

The possibility to access a broad network, to pool and maximize resources, and to access providers with both elasticity and scalability while also containing costs ought to be put together with the mitigation of their authorized compliance risks. In this respect, cloud computing presents inherent dangers concerning the security of personal data processed from the cloud. The European Data Protection authorities group the main risks related to privacy and personal data protection in the cloud into two categories (Article 29 Working Party 2012, pp. 5–6):

1. Lack of control over personal data
2. Lack of information on the processing of personal data

For that reason, the trade-off between the expected advantages of outsourcing to cloud providers and the risks for personal data in the cloud should be considered by organizations before purchasing cloud services (ENISA 2009, "Cloud Computing Risk Assesment").

14.2.4.   OUTSOURCING CLOUD SERVICES

Those who purchase cloud services should always first go through both an external and internal due diligence check. The following aspects should be considered in the due diligence check. Tables 14.1 and 14.2, the internal

Table 14.1. Internal due diligence checklist

1. Define cloud client privacy, security, and compliance requirements.
2. Identify what data, processes, or services a cloud client wants to move to the cloud.
3. Analyze the risks of outsourcing services to the cloud.
4. Identify the security controls needed to protect personal data once transferred to the cloud.
5. Define responsibilities.

Table 14.2. External due diligence checklist

1. Assess whether the provider meets its privacy and data protection requirements using, for example, the PLAs V2 (Cloud Security Alliance 2015).

2. Check whether the provider holds any certification or attestation released by an independent third party.

3. Consider whether the terms of service can be amended, how and by whom.

4. Understand whether and how the security controls implemented by the provider can be monitored.

and external due diligence checklists, respectively, identify a list of considerations that the customer should look at attentively when contemplating a cloud purchase.

14.2.5. STEP 2: MAJOR ISSUES IN ENTERING A CLOUD SERVICE CONTRACT

Entering into a cloud contract, like any other type of arrangement, presents the customer with many issues that must be carefully considered including jurisdiction and applicable law and privacy roles. These considerations will be discussed below in depth.

14.2.6. JURISDICTION AND APPLICABLE LAW

Clauses are often present in cloud service contracts that allow for the competent jurisdiction and applicable law to be established in the agreement between the two parties. The establishment of the relevant authority intends the allocation of the power to enforce the contract to a specific competent judge, while the setting of the applicable law means the establishment of the rules applicable to the agreement. In theory, the principle of contractual liberty grants the parties the possibility to agree on and establish the jurisdiction and the applicable law to the contract. In practice, however, the cloud service provider is the entity that decides the competent forum and the applicable law, leaving little negotiation power to the client. Concerning applicable privacy law, the Data Protection Directive 95/46/EC on the protection of individuals concerning the processing of personal data and the free movement of such data applies when personal data are processed as a result of the utilization of cloud computing technology services.

The e-privacy Directive 2002/58/ EC,[5] the application of which is triggered by the provision of publicly available electronic communications services in public communications networks (e.g., telecom operators) by way of the cloud, should also be considered here. In fact, this law plays a role when either the cloud client or the cloud provider falls under the definition of a provider of publicly available electronic communications services in public communications networks. The guidelines for determining the applicable law for the processing of personal data performed by a cloud computing service provider is outlined in Article 4 of Directive 95/46/EC, differentiating between EU-based controllers and those located outside the EU. When the data controller[6] is based in the EU, the applicable law is one of the EU member states where it is established. On the contrary, when different establishments of the same controller are present, the applicable law is that of each of the EU member state in which the processing of personal data occurs.[7] For controllers located outside the EU that make use of automated equipment in an EU member state's territory, the law of the latter is applicable unless the computer is only used for transit. Therefore, if a cloud client is located outside the EU but procures cloud services from a provider located within the EU, the provider "exports" the data protection legislation to the client itself. Clients should carefully examine both the jurisdiction and the applicable law in their decision-making process as illustrated in Table 14.3.

Table 14.3. Jurisdiction and applicable law

1. The contractual arrangements regarding the jurisdiction and the applicable law to the contract are found in the cloud service agreement.
2. In the EU, the relevant privacy law is the one of the EU member state where the data controller is located, which, in principle, means the law of the country where the cloud client resides.

---

[5]Directive 2002/58/EC of the European Parliament and of the Council of July 12, 2002 concerning the processing of personal data and the protection of privacy in the electronic communications sector—Directive on privacy and electronic communications—and subsequent amendments (http://eur-lex.europa.eu/LexUriServ/LexUriServ.do?uri=CELEX:32002L0058:en:HTML) applies to "the processing of personal data in connection with the provision of publicly available electronic communications services in public communications networks in the Community" (Article 3.1). More precisely, as per Article 1, "Scope and aim 1. This Directive harmonises the provisions of the Member States required to ensure an equivalent level of protection of fundamental rights and freedoms, and in particular the right to privacy, with respect to the processing of personal data in the electronic communication sector and to ensure the free movement of such data and of electronic communication equipment and services in the Community. 2. The provisions of this Directive particularise and complement Directive 95/46/EC for the purposes mentioned in paragraph 1."
[6]The data controller is usually the client of a cloud provider.
[7]It is useful to read Article 17.3 of Directive 95/46/EC, stipulating that the law regulating the security measures of a data processing agreement is that of the EU member state in which the processor is established.

Table 14.4. Privacy role aspects for the cloud customer to consider

1. Transparently allocate the data protection roles.
2. Choose a cloud service provider that guarantees compliance with European Data Protection law.
3. Determine the degree of autonomy of the cloud service provider acting as data processor regarding the methods and technical or organizational measures to be adopted.
4. Bind the cloud service provider operating as a data processor utilizing a specific data processing agreement or establish the clearly defined boundaries of data processing in the cloud service agreement and ensure that the activities outsourced to the cloud service provider are adequately circumscribed.
5. Avoid using providers who use a complex data processing flow.

14.2.7. PRIVACY ROLES

It is essential that the privacy roles in data processing through the cloud are transparent for the legal obligations and responsibilities of the parties to the contract to be correctly allocated. The standard allocation of duties (Article 29 Working Party 2012, p. 7) demonstrates that the controllership of personal data processed in the cloud belongs to the client. On the contrary, the cloud service provider is regularly considered to be the data processor. The cloud client, as data controller, accepts responsibility for data protection regulation compliance, insofar as the same is responsible and subject to all the legal duties outlined in Directive 95/46/EC. Instead, the cloud provider has some leeway in the definition of the methods and the technical or organizational measures to be used to achieve the purposes of the controller. Table 14.5 acts as a checklist, outlining aspects to be taken into consideration by the cloud customer.

Table 14.5. Amendments to the contract checklist

- Contracts should dictate the services provided and under what conditions, including procedural ones; these can be modified in the course of the provision of services.
- Changes that could prove detrimental to the level of a mission-critical service and the level of protection of personal data should be excluded in the contract itself.
- Notice should be given to the client before making changes.
- The client's right to prior notification of any changes to the agreement can be included in the contract.
- The client should verify whether the contract provides them with the right to terminate the contract should unwanted, or unnoticed issues.

14.2.8. AMENDMENTS TO THE CONTRACT

Cloud providers often retain the right to unilaterally change cloud contracts themselves, adding specific clauses permitting this in the cloud contracts. This represents a significant problem for the client who must then verify if the contract foresees notice from the provider in these circumstances or allows the client to terminate the contract in light of detrimental changes to it. Table 14.5 lays out many suggestions for cloud customers concerning amendments to the cloud contract.

14.2.9. DATA LOCATION AND TRANSFERS OF DATA

Cloud computing often entails that data are processed or located on servers outside the EU, and therefore the transfer of personal data outside the EU is highly likely. It is essential to pay particular attention to the flow of personal data in cloud contracts. As outlined in the European Commission Decisions on the Adequacy of the Protection of Personal Data in Third Countries, Directive 95/46/EC forbids the transfer of personal data to third countries that do not ensure an adequate level of protection for personal data.[8] According to Article 25 (6),

> the Commission may find (. . .) that a third country ensures an adequate level of protection, by reason of its domestic law or of the international commitments it has entered into, particularly upon conclusion of the negotiations (with the Commission), for the protection of the private lives and basic freedoms and rights of individuals.[4]

Personal data may be transferred to countries not offering an adequate level of protection when:

1. At least one of the conditions listed in Article 26 (1) is fulfilled.*
2. The recipients of personal data sign the standard model clauses approved by the European Commission.[4]
3. The recipient organization participates in the binding corporate rules adopted by the EU Data Protection Authorities in place.[9]

---

[8]See in this respect, Privacy level agreement [V2]: A compliance tool for providing cloud services in the European Union, available at https://cloudsecurityalliance.org/download/privacy-level-agreement-version-2/ ISO/IEC 27018; http://www.iso.org/iso/catalogue_detail.htm?csnumber=61498; the Cloud service level agreement standardisation guidelines, available at https://ec.europa.eu/digital-agenda/en/news/cloud-servicelevel-agreement-standardisation-guidelines; the work developed by the Cloud Select Industry Group on the code of conduct, available at HTTP://ec.europa.eu/digital-agenda/en/cloud-select-industry-group-code-conduct; the Cloud accountability

[9]The complete list of Commission's decisions finding an adequate level of protection in third countries for personal data is available at http://ec.europa.eu/justice/data-protection/document/international-transfers/adequacy/index_en.htm

The transfer of data to organizations established in the United States is possible when they are safe harbor certified.[10] When the processing of personal data occurs in countries that do not offer adequate safeguards, it is recommended to sign the model clauses adopted by the Commission (Decision 2010/87/EU) between the client (controller/exporter of data) and the provider (processor/importer). Furthermore, personal data can be transferred outside the EU when at least one of the conditions listed above is fulfilled in the contract (e.g., Article 26.1 of the Directive applies or adheres to safe harbor protocol).

14.2.10. PROCESSING OF PERSONAL DATA BY SUBCONTRACTORS

Providers of cloud services may outsource some of the processing for the functioning of the cloud to subcontractors. Such subcontractors, which may be located outside the EU, receive personal data from cloud service clients. The same is allowed to process personal data from the EU in a lawful way only when at least one of the conditions in the previous paragraphs is met. Moreover, it is important to realize that multiple different subprocessors may be engaged, possibly resulting in the loss of control over personal data and lack of accountability of the data processing, and therefore prove difficult for the data subject to exercise his or her rights. The cloud customer should examine the considerations that follow in Table 14.6.

Table 14.6. Subprocessors and subcontractors

1. In Opinion 5/2012 (Article 29 Working Party 2012, pp. 9–10, 20), the European Data Protection authorities recommended that processors (providers) inform clients of the subprocessing in place, thereby specifying the type of service subcontracted, the characteristics of current or potential subcontractors, and that such entities guarantee compliance with Directive 95/46/EC.

2. The cloud provider must ensure that its subcontractors are contractually bound by the same obligations and standards agreed upon with the controller. The model contractual clauses approved by the European Commission are useful in this case.

3. The controller should possess contractual recourses for the processor in case of any breach of the contract caused by the subprocessor.

---

[10]Read more about BCRs at https://ec.europa.eu/info/law/law-topic/data-protection/data-transfers-outside-eu/rules-international-transfers-personal-data_en § Regarding safe harbor, see the official program's website at https://2016.export.gov/safeharbor/ Sole self-certification with safe harbor may not be deemed sufficient in the absence of robust enforcement of data protection principles in the cloud environment. See Opinion 05/2012 on cloud computing, p. 17. Also read Decisions 2001/497/EC and 2004/915/EC concerning transfers from controllers to controllers and Decision 2010/87/EU (repealing Decision 2002/16/EC) for transfers from controllers to processors, available at https://europa.eu/european-union/contact/data-protection_en

14.2.11. DATA SUBJECTS' RIGHTS (INTERVENABILITY)

Under Directive 95/46/EC, data subjects have the right of access, right of rectification, right of erasure, right of blocking, and right of objection. The client should always control if the provider guarantees full cooperation in the granting of easy-to-exercise rights of the data subject, even when subcontractors further process data. Also, the client should make sure that in the contract the cloud provider explicitly undertakes to cooperate with the cloud client to ensure an effective exercise of data subjects' rights, even when subcontractors further process data.

14.2.12. STEP 3: EXITING A CLOUD SERVICE CONTRACT: MAJOR ISSUES

The third step examines the major issues to be considered when exiting a cloud service contract. Lock-in and interoperability, SLAs, and termination of the agreement will be discussed.

14.2.13. LOCK-IN AND INTEROPERABILITY

Lock-in can be a consequence of the utilization of proprietary data formats and service interfaces on the part of the cloud provider, rendering the interoperability and portability of data from a cloud provider very difficult. Lack of interoperability and portability inevitably make the migration of services more complicated (lock-in effect). The client should follow the two suggestions laid out in Table 14.7.

Table 14.7. Lock-in and interoperability checklist

- Check whether and how the cloud provider ensures data portability and interoperability.
- Choose standard data formats and service interfaces facilitating interoperability.

14.2.14. SERVICE-LEVEL AGREEMENTS

SLAs form an integral part of cloud computing contracts. SLAs help cloud clients identify the services and the service-level objectives that the cloud provider offers. SLAs are expressed concerning metrics on the performance of the services, and so they are usually measured in numbers.

SLAs can vary drastically from provider to provider. Both at the European and international levels, initiatives have attempted to standardize SLAs between providers.[11] SLAs can define the performance of the services, for example, concerning the availability of the service, the security, and the way in which data are managed, as well as sometimes including personal data protection provisions. The client should always:

1. Carefully read and analyze the SLAs.
2. Check whether the cloud service agreement provides for service credits and remedies to service-level breaches, for example, monetary compensation.

14.2.15. TERMINATION OF THE CONTRACT

During the termination phase of a cloud contract, the client must be able to retrieve the data that were transferred to the cloud. This must be done within a specific period before the provider proceeds to delete the same data. Two useful tips can be found in Table 14.8. Further input and

Table 14.8. Suggestions: Termination of the contract

• The steps of the termination process should be identified in the cloud agreement.
• A good cloud agreement should contain provisions regulating the data retrieval time, for example, the time in which clients can retrieve a copy of their data from the cloud service. The data retention period should also be included, as well as the procedures followed by the provider to transfer personal data back to the client or to allow the latter to migrate to another provider later on.

guidance specifically related to personal data protection compliance can be found in the previously cited PLA V2, of which the writer was the principal author. PLA V2 acts as an appendix to cloud services agreements to describe what levels of privacy protection the cloud provider provides as opposed to SLAs, which provide metrics and information concerning the performance of services (Cloud Security Alliance 2015).

---

[11]See the DG CONNECT initiative establishing the Cloud Select Industry Group—Subgroup on Service-Level Agreements (C-SIG-SLA) for the development of standardization guidelines for cloud computing SLAs. More information can be found at https://ec.europa.eu/digital-agenda/en/news/cloud-service-level-agreement-standardisation-guidelines

In a PLA V2, the cloud provider describes the privacy and data protection standards that it promises to maintain during the data processing, potentially promoting a significant global rule for the cloud provider.

PLA V2 is a work that fits under Key Action 2 Safe and Fair Contract Terms and Conditions outlined in the communication from the Commission to the European Parliament, the Council, and the European Economic and Social Committee of the Regions. According to the European Cloud Strategy,

> Identifying and disseminating best practices in respect of model contract terms will accelerate the take-up of cloud computing by increasing the trust of prospective customers. Appropriate actions on contract terms can also help in the crucial area of data protection. Develop with stakeholders model terms for cloud computing service level agreements for contracts between cloud providers and professional cloud users. (European Commission 2012)

This chapter has provided the reader with tips and recommendations to be considered in the cloud relationship during the precontractual, contractual, and postcontractual phases. Before moving to the cloud, in fact, potential clients should always ensure they have found a cloud provider that offers an adequate level of data protection, making an informed decision to procure services from the cloud provider offering the highest safeguards (Cloud Security Alliance 2015). Some cloud providers fail to be transparent and all too often have unreasonable limitations and exclusions of liability clauses in their conditions of service. Making an informed decision upon procurement, however, is not enough. Clients must also regularly ensure that the selected cloud provider abides by data protection compliance controls, even taking into consideration the limitations and exclusions of liability clauses. Cloud customers, namely businesses and public administrations, need to put increased focus on the cloud service agreement, making sure that it meets the relevant legal compliance requirements and that the duties and obligations of both parties are established.

Article 29 Working Party Opinion 5/2012 provides a checklist that proves useful in cloud procurement, stating that the legal certainty, security, and transparency of the client should be critical determinants in the provision of cloud services (Article 29 Working Party 2012). For that reason, tools such as the PLA V2 can be beneficial, representing structured disclosure forms for cloud providers and therefore allowing them to be fully transparent regarding their privacy policies, allowing customers to compare cloud providers and make informed decisions quickly.

As previously underlined, the exponential growth of cloud computing is changing the way that businesses and governments both think and function. The growth of the cloud will inevitably continue at an even faster rate than what we have seen to date, making the understanding of how cloud contracts work increasingly important.

REFERENCES

Anderson, E., L. Lai-ling, Y. Dharmasthira, C. Eschinger, S. Cournoyer, C. Tornbohm, J. Roster, B. Granetto, G. Tramacere, D. Blackmore, J.M. Correia, L. Wurster, T. Eid, R. Contu, V. Liu, F. Biscotti, C. Pang, D. Sommer, T.J. Singh, A. Frank, H. Swinehart, A. Dayley, J. Zhang, M. Yeates, R. Kandaswamy, D. Toombs, and G. Petri. 2013. "Forecast: Public Cloud Services, Worldwide, 2011–2017, 4Q13 Update." *Gartner*. www.gartner.com/doc/2642020/forecast-public-cloudservices-worldwide

Article 29 Data Protection Working Party. 2012. "Opinion 05/2012 on Cloud Computing." European Commission, Brussels.

Asia Cloud Computing Association. 2015. The Launch of the Asia Cloud Computing Association's New Research Report Asia's Financial Services: Ready for the Cloud—A Report on FSI Regulations Impacting Cloud in Asia-Pacific Markets. http://www.asiacloudcomputing.org/research/fsi

Bradshaw, S., C. Millard, and I. Walden. 2010. "Contracts for Clouds: Comparison and Analysis of the Terms and Conditions of Cloud Computing Services." Legal Studies Research Paper No. 63/2010, Queen Mary University of London, School of Law, London. SSRN. http://ssrn.com/abstract=1662374 or http://dx.doi.org/10.2139/ssrn.1662374

Cloud Security Alliance. 2015. "Privacy Level Agreement [V2]: A Compliance Tool for Providing Cloud Services in the European Union." https://cloudsecurityalliance.org/download/privacy-level-agreement-version-2/

CloudWATCH. 2014. "D3.5 Legal Guide to the Cloud: How to Protect Personal Data in Cloud Service Contracts."

Digital Agenda for Europe. 2014. "Cloud Service Level Agreement Standardisation Guidelines."

ENISA. 2009. "Cloud Computing Risk Assesment". https://www.enisa.europa.eu/news/enisa-news/enisa-2009-report-on-cloud-computing-now-available-in-italian

EUR-Lex. 1995. Directive 95/46/EC of the European Parliament and of the Council of 24 October 1995 on the Protection of Individuals About the Processing of Personal Data and the Free Movement of Such Data, *Official Journal L* 281, pp. 31–50.

European Commission. 2012. "Unleashing the Potential of Cloud Computing in Europe (COM(2012) 529 final)." http://eur-lex.europa.eu/LexUriServ/LexUriServ.do?uri=COM:2012:0529:FIN:EN:PDF

Eurostat. 2014. "Cloud Computing—Statistics on the Use by Enterprises." http://ec.europa.eu/eurostat/statistics-explained/index.php/Cloud_computing_-_statistics_on_the_use_by_enterprises

Gartner. 2013. "Gartner Identifies the Top 10 Strategic Technology Trends for 2014." Web. 6 July 2015.

Helberger, N., and L. Verite. 2014. "EU Cloud Computing Expert Group: Discussion Paper Pre-Contractual Information Requirements and Cloud Services." European Commission. https://ec.europa.eu/info/law/law-topic/consumers/consumer-contracts-law_en

Hon, W.K., C. Millard, and I. Walden. 2012. "Negotiating Cloud Contracts—Looking at Clouds from Both Sides Now." *Stanford Technology Law Review* 16, p. 81. http://www.cloudlegal.ccls.qmul.ac.uk/research/our-research-papers/cloud-contracts/negotiating-cloud-contracts-looking-at-clouds-from-both-sides-now/

Kundra, V. 2011. "The Federal Cloud Computing Strategy." Washington, DC: The White House. https://www.whitehouse.gov/sites/default/files/omb/assets/egov_docs/federal-cloud-computing-strategy.pdf

OECD. 2014. "Cloud Computing: The Concept, Impacts and the Role of Government Policy," OECD Digital Economy Papers, No. 240. Paris, France: OECD Publishing.

CHAPTER 15

FUTURE DIRECTIONS IN CLOUD COMPUTING SECURITY

Unlike the previous attempts to introduce computing as a service, cloud computing has been successful in various domains of computing with a rapidly growing market for cloud-based services. With its convenient pay-as-you-go service, low-cost computing offers, and flexible but infinite infrastructure resources, cloud computing is highly likely to be one of the major computing paradigms in the future. As reported by Gartner Inc., a US-based information technology research and advisory firm, 2016 will be the defining year for cloud computing to emerge, and nearly half of the large enterprises will engage with cloud-based deployments by the end of 2017. Government sectors, which were relatively reluctant to adopt cloud-based solutions due to security concerns, are also becoming interested and are predicted to switch to the cloud. Security is a major concern for distributed systems and services.

Cloud computing has inherited all these security issues from its predecessors. Moreover, the new concepts introduced by cloud computing, such as computation outsourcing, resource sharing, and external data warehousing, increased the privacy concerns and made cloud computing platforms prone to newer security issues and threats. Therefore, security in cloud-based solutions is highly crucial and may be considered as one of the most significant barriers to widespread adoption and acceptance. The 2014 iCloud data breach demonstrated the vulnerability and insecurity of cloud computing. Cloud computing not only introduces additional risks and challenges but also adds various complications to deploying and maintaining the existing security standards. Widespread mobile device access and the on-demand services offered by cloud providers amplify the security concerns and threats even further. Table 15.1

Table 15.1. Known attacks against cloud computing

Attack	Consequence	Category
• Theft of service • Denial of service • Malware injection • Cross virtual machine side-channel • Targeted shared memory • Phishing • Botnets • Virtual machine rollback attack	• Service theft • Service unavailability • Information leakage • Cloud malware injection • Unauthorized access • Malware injection • Launching brute-force attack • Leakage of sensitive information	• Cloud infrastructure • Access control

lists some of the known attacks and their consequences. According to US law, information security is defined as the protection of information and information systems from unauthorized access, use, disclosure, disruption, modification, inspection, recording, or destruction to provide integrity, confidentiality, and availability of information. Therefore, to be endured in time, cloud computing should address all of these security issues beforehand. Gartner Inc. has proposed seven primary cloud computing security risks: outsourcing services, regulatory compliance, data location, shared environment, business continuity and disaster recovery, hard environment for investigating illegal activity, and long-term viability. A categorized discussion on cloud security issues is presented in Section 15.1.

15.1. CATEGORIES

Security issues may be raised in different layers in the cloud computing model. There are system-level threats, where an intruder bypasses the security to get unauthorized access, as well as cloud infrastructure and network-level threats. Each component of a cloud should be separately addressed and requires equal attention to protect a cloud computing platform as a whole. As discussed, Cloud Security categories can be categorized into four categories shown in Table 15.2. These categories are

Table 15.2. Cloud security categories

Data outsourcing	Integrity, confidentiality, authenticity, storage, transfer, and migration of data
Access control	User-level authentication and authorization of resources
Infrastructure	Virtualization, network, and platform-level security issues
Security standards	Standards and regulations for SLAs, auditing, implementation, and service descriptions

closely related in various aspects. Whenever one category is vulnerable to a certain attack, other categories also fail to ensure the desired security. Therefore, suitable management and security precautions in one category strengthen the other categories even more and may eliminate the subsequent threats. Thus, security research in cloud computing should address the complete set of issues in a holistic approach, instead of an iterative or categorical resolution of threats.

ABOUT THE AUTHOR

Giulio D'Agostino is a system administrator, entrepreneur and cyber security consultant with more than twenty years' experience in the cloud computing, software as a service, and publishing fields. Previously employed by Google, Apple, Hewlett Packard and Salesforce.com, Giulio has lectured at the Technical University of Denmark – DTU, Griffith College Dublin, Web Summit 2016/2017, worked as Irish Tech News contributor and he is currently working as system administrator for SaaS and cloud-based remote connectivity services company LogMeIn Inc.

INDEX

FORTHCOMING TITLES FROM OUR COMPUTER ENGINEERING FOUNDATIONS, CURRENTS, AND TRAJECTORIES COLLECTION

Lisa McLean, *Editor*

- *Data Security in Cloud Computing, Volume I* by Giulio D'Agostino
- *Advanced Selenium Web Accessibility Testing: Software Automation Testing Secrets Revealed* by Narayanan Palani

Momentum Press is one of the leading book publishers in the field of engineering, mathematics, health, and applied sciences. Momentum Press offers over 30 collections, including Aerospace, Biomedical, Civil, Environmental, Nanomaterials, Geotechnical, and many others.

Momentum Press is actively seeking collection editors as well as authors. For more information about becoming an MP author or collection editor, please visit http://www.momentumpress.net/contact

Announcing Digital Content Crafted by Librarians

Concise e-books business students need for classroom and research

Momentum Press offers digital content as authoritative treatments of advanced engineering topics by leaders in their field. Hosted on ebrary, MP provides practitioners, researchers, faculty, and students in engineering, science, and industry with innovative electronic content in sensors and controls engineering, advanced energy engineering, manufacturing, and materials science.

Momentum Press offers library-friendly terms:
- *perpetual access for a one-time fee*
- *no subscriptions or access fees required*
- *unlimited concurrent usage permitted*
- *downloadable PDFs provided*
- *free MARC records included*
- *free trials*

The **Momentum Press** digital library is very affordable, with no obligation to buy in future years.

For more information, please visit **www.momentumpress.net/library** or to set up a trial in the US, please contact **mpsales@globalepress.com**.